DATE DUE

DEMCO 38-296

AUDUBON:
NATURAL PRIORITIES

by Roger DiSilvestro
Executive Editor—Christopher Palmer

Turner Publishing, Inc.
ATLANTA

Published by Turner Publishing, Inc.
A Subsidiary of Turner Broadcasting System, Inc.
1050 Techwood Drive, N.W.
Atlanta, Georgia 30318

Distributed by Andrews and McMeel
A Universal Press Syndicate Company
4900 Main Street
Kansas City, Missouri 64112

Library of Congress Cataloging-in-Publication Data
DiSilvestro, Roger L.
    Audubon : natural priorities / by Roger DiSilvestro. — 1st ed.
        p.   cm.
    Includes bibliographical references and index.
    ISBN 1-878685-51-1 : $24.95
    1. Environmental policy—United States—History. 2. Environmental
protection—United States—History. 3. Social ecology—United
States—History. I. Title.
GE180.D57 1993
333.95'16'0973—dc20   94-18452
                                                             CIP

EDITOR—Crawford Barnett
COPY EDITOR—Lauren Emerson
ART DIRECTOR—Elaine Streithof
PRODUCTION MANAGER—Christine Holmes
PHOTO EDITOR—Marty Moore

First Edition 10 9 8 7 6 5 4 3 2 1
Printed in the U.S.A. on Recycled Paper.

CONTENTS

Foreword

BY
CHRISTOPHER N. PALMER
EXECUTIVE PRODUCER, *WORLD OF AUDUBON SPECIALS*
AND
PRESIDENT, NATIONAL AUDUBON SOCIETY PRODUCTIONS

Audubon: Natural Priorities, together with the 1994 World of Audubon anniversary special, is the cumulative result of an exciting and productive ten-year partnership between the National Audubon Society and Turner Broadcasting.

This partnership has produced dozens of award-winning television documentaries, an Emmy-winning children's television show, books, interactive multimedia programs, music videos, computer software, a motion picture, and much more.

The reach of our television programs never ceases to amaze me. In 1993, I received a note from Sandy Sprunt, an Audubon scientist, who had just returned from leading an Audubon expedition to Trinidad and Venezuela. The route in Venezuela was up the Orinoco River into the deep rain forest, where the group spent a couple of days at a remote camp. Sandy wrote me: "On one of our trips by dugout canoe, the guide saw my cap, which had an Audubon patch on it. He made a special effort to tell me that he very much liked and appreciated our Audubon Specials on TBS—they have satellite dishes, even in the jungle."

When we started this television series in the mid-1980s, environmental issues were much in the news. However, no one had ever produced a long-running television series that regularly examined environmental and conservation issues in depth. Filling the void was the idea behind the *World of Audubon Specials*. We set out to produce a TV series that revealed environmental and conservation problems and outlined solutions, while at the same time offering entertainment for the entire family.

The Audubon Television Department was staffed not by

TV producers creating nature films, but by professional environmentalists determined to harness the power of television and other electronic media to achieve the advocacy goals of the National Audubon Society with intelligence and passion. This focus set us apart from other nature programming, which concentrates mainly on natural history while ignoring the political and social issues surrounding wildlife and the use of wildlands. For the past decade, Audubon TV has remained the only television series in the world that deals exclusively with environmental and wildlife policy issues.

The Audubon Television Specials play a role in the global effort to restore natural ecosystems and the Earth's biological diversity. Through the programs, we at Audubon want to stimulate citizen action for environmentally sustainable development, which is to say that we underscore the need to use resources without losing them. We want our shows to empower viewers, to make them more active on environmental and conservation issues, to increase their involvement in recycling, in writing to elected officials, in participating in local programs, and in voting.

This involvement is crucial to both human and wildlife survival, as this book illustrates. But if environmental concerns are to receive broad public support, involvement must come from a far larger constituency than "card-carrying" environmentalists can compose. Consequently, a fundamental purpose of the Audubon TV documentaries is to build public support for environmental issues by introducing millions of viewers to the ecological arena and showing them that concern about the natural world is relevant to their lives.

To do this, the Audubon Specials combine cutting-edge information and issues with portraits of interesting characters set in dramatic stories hosted by celebrities who have a personal commitment to the issues the programs explore. With the political and scientific expertise of my Audubon colleagues, the creative expertise of our filmmakers, the caring participation of concerned celebrities, and the loyal and indefatigable support of Ted Turner, we have been able to offer millions of viewers vital information that they can use for taking action on critical issues.

The programs have covered a wide diversity of subjects, from the vital significance of ecosystem conservation to the protection of individual species. They have visited sites as far flung as the Galápagos Islands, Africa, and the Arctic coast. They have revealed problems in the heart of the nation, such as the decline of wetlands and rivers in the Midwest and the near biological destruction of the Great Lakes. They have examined problems such as pollution and overpopulation. They have shown the destruction that has been wrought on ancient forests and ocean shores. In doing all this, I know the National Audubon Society has been both a pillar for its allies and a thorn in the side of its opponents.

I know this because I witnessed the reactions to our programs on logging in the Pacific Northwest and livestock grazing on public lands. These programs led ranching and lumber advocates to boycott the advertisers who bought commercial time during the Audubon Specials. These boycotts were an attempt to stifle our programs before they aired, in fact, before the boycotters themselves even saw the shows and knew their content. All advertisers fled from the film *Rage Over Trees*, which examined the logging industry. Ted Turner, never one to succumb to political pressure, aired the program several times without advertiser support.

The boycotts were organized by so-called wise-use groups, which receive millions of dollars in support from timber, mining, and oil companies, off-road vehicle manufacturers, and other industries that profit from exploitation of public lands, often with little or no concern for proper stewardship of our national resources. The wise-use movement seeks to reverse virtually every environmental advance our nation has made in the past quarter century. Two leaders of the movement devoted virtually an entire chapter in their 1993 book, *Trashing the Economy*, to complaining about the power of Audubon's television programming. I take this as a sign of our success and significance.

On the positive side, I think of an Audubon member who in September 1993 wrote to tell me that he uses the Audubon Special *The New Range Wars* in the high school science classes in teaches in Carlsbad, New Mexico. Even in this case, local opposition is trying to choke off communication. As the letter states: "Ranchers have called the principal, School Board members, and the superintendent demanding that the video be banned from further showing in the school system and that steps be taken to insure that a video of this type never be shown in the school again. At this point it appears that the principal may in fact ban the video. . . . What is the best tactic to fight this 1993 version of Nazi book burners?"

His question suggests to me that although we have had a successful ten years, our work has just begun. I hope our programs will continue for another ten years, and for decades after that, shedding light on important environmental issues and arming citizens with the information they need to combat stranglers of the free exchange of ideas.

In the future, urgent environmental problems will continue to threaten both the populations and the ecosystems of our planet. Audubon is dedicated to continuing the fight against these assaults in the hope that natural ecosystems and the Earth's biological diversity can be restored.

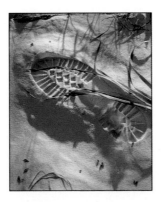

Introduction

Don't Save the Earth

Some say the world will end in fire, some say in ice, and some, from the scientific community, say it will end in about eight billion years, when the sun explodes and vaporizes the planet. Others say that, long before the sun self-destructs, humanity will destroy the Earth, at least as we know it.

Even if the last scenario proves correct, life *will* continue. Nature, through the process of evolution, produces prodigious quantities of life. Scientists have identified millions of species of plants and animals and expect to discover as many as twenty million more. But these are not the first species to have lived upon our planet. Several times in the past, millions of species evolved, only to be nearly wiped out by catastrophic events, the details of which remain hidden in the fossil records that remain. After these extinctions, life slowly recovered. Indeed, evidence suggests that eradications stimulate evolution, allowing for the rapid emergence and increased dominance of many species. Consider mammals, the warm-blooded class of creatures that includes humans. For millions of years mammals lived without making much of a mark on prehistory, probably because the dinosaurs were so successful that few could compete against them. Then something wiped out the dinosaurs, and mammals gave rise to many new species that achieved a new prominence.

So, while it is true that human development is destroying species at an unprecedented rate, this extinction event will not destroy the Earth. What, then, is the environmental movement about? Why be concerned about the big environmental issues—global warming, overpopulation, deforestation, desertification, species extinctions—why be concerned, if not to save the Earth? The answer is simple: to save ourselves.

All creatures alter their environment—it is unavoidable in the struggle for survival—but humans have taken change to

Life-giving thunderheads break up, allowing the sun's last rays to shine through at Everglades National Park. South Florida's drought-drown cycle feeds the park in the rainy season, leaving it an oasis in the dry winter. This vital pattern has been disrupted by agriculture and other human activities, throwing the survival of many species into question. (facing page)

a new quantum level. Thanks to our ever-increasing technological abilities, we have transformed the world more pro-
foundly than any other species. In general, we have tried to
modify it in ways that make it more beneficial to us. The
problem is that we cannot be certain that the changes we
bring do not pose long-term threats.

Humans, like all living things, are adapted to their environment. As creatures that evolved in tropical climes perhaps five million years ago, we do best in warm areas. We
think of the Arctic as inhospitable because we need so many
support systems to survive in it. We need to insulate ourselves from that frozen world or we will die. Our ability to
adapt to such areas through technology allows us to live well
beyond the parts of the globe to which we are biologically
adapted.

But in the end, even technological adaptation has its limits. Despite the advances we have made, we still need food,
water, air, and space to live in. Evolution has equipped us to
live in the world as we know it. We may, however, find ourselves unable to survive if the world is changed so greatly
that our biological needs can no longer be met.

The environmental movement seeks to bring some element of thought and control to humanity's rampant charge
across the globe. It seeks to limit the changes technology
brings to the natural workings of the planet. It seeks to keep
the Earth in a state that will support human life. The environmental movement's concern about saving endangered
species, keeping rivers, lakes, and seas clean, slowing the
effects of global warming, stabilizing human populations, and
preserving natural ecosystems all boils down to a simple
desire to preserve the world as a place in which we can live
happily and successfully.

The environmental movement has received a great deal of
attention from the press in recent years, and the public has
grown increasingly interested in environmental issues. A
recent Roper poll revealed that 57 percent of the American
people think endangered species should be protected even if
that protection is costly. Fully 35 percent think endangered
species should be protected at any cost.

Nevertheless, the environmental movement has found

itself increasingly involved in disputes over the use of natural resources and the need for environmental protections. This occurs in part because industrial society is poised on a cusp. For the first time in history we understand the devastating effect many of our actions have on the environment, and we know the threats this devastation poses to our own survival. At the same time, many forces in our society, notably the big corporations, are still behind the times in reconciling the issue of immediate profit versus long-term survival. In effect, scientific knowledge is still trickling down to the business interests that play such a large role in shaping national policies. Society is in the midst of a sea of change as it shifts from development conducted with little or no environmental concern to development tempered by environmental awareness.

This may seem a daunting task, but today we have means for creating environmental awareness that previous generations lacked. The National Wildlife Federation's *Conservation Directory* lists more than six hundred private conservation groups dedicated to calling attention to environmental issues. Not only do the biggest of these groups publish magazines, books, newsletters, and brochures; they also produce films, computer software, and television programs about ecological problems and solutions, providing a wide range of media through which the public can receive information. The increasing availability of knowledge represents promise for widespread awareness. The growing environmental concern of recent years represents a fruition of the work these groups have accomplished during the past century and portends a brighter ecological future.

These groups offer each of us, as individuals, the means for changing our own behavior so that we can become more environmentally responsible. Also, by uniting our many voices into a single powerful chorus, they offer us a chance to participate in the shaping of public policy. Although the problems the environmental movement, and indeed all of us, face today are far more complicated and challenging than those confronted by any previous generation, we are better equipped to recognize the need for environmental responsibility and to accept it.

Chapter One

The Conservation Movement is Born

When Columbus first set his sails westward, he was looking not for strange new worlds but for Asia, and the reason was commerce. When he made his first landfall in the Caribbean in 1492, he found the islands there already settled by people he mistakenly called Indians, on the assumption that he had reached his original destination. In short order, he and his men plundered the Indians' villages for gold and other lucre and took the Indians themselves as slaves, thus setting a precedent for Europeans who came later.

Those who did follow came, like Columbus, in search of trade goods. They found them in the rich forests of eastern North America, in the grasslands of the Southwest, in the rich trapping grounds along rivers and lakes, replete with beaver and other furbearers. The Pilgrims themselves came in 1620 as a commercial venture, traveling on borrowed cash. Few explorers sought to study the new land and its abundant resources. Most simply wanted to make quick money, and they acted accordingly.

The emphasis on profit to the exclusion of all other interests proved fatal for many natural resources. In the area that would become the United States, forests were quickly felled and wild animals were slaughtered for their meat and hides. By 1646, English colonists had so reduced New England's deer population that Rhode Island initiated the continent's first closed hunting season in an effort to spare the remaining deer. Nevertheless, at the end of the 1600s, Virginia and the Carolinas were still sending roughly 150,000 deer hides to England every year.

Of course, market hunters were not killing only deer. They were, in effect, killing everything. In the East, they wiped out populations of elk, caribou, and moose. Ducks, geese, swans, many species of shorebirds, and even songbirds were decimated for the meat markets. At the start of the

The arrival of explorers in the New World inaugurated five hundred years of exploitation. America was a land of plenty, and for centuries it was treated as if its resources were unending. In the late 1800s small groups of people began to see the destructive path the nation was on, and their efforts gave birth to what has become modern conservation. (facing page)

nineteenth century, many commercial hunters shifted their attention to the West, their rifles tearing into the millions of bison and pronghorn antelope that roamed the plains and prairies, cutting down the hundreds of thousands of elk, deer, and wild sheep that lived among the bison, and nearly wiping out the wolves, mountain lions, and grizzly bears that preyed upon the grassland herbivores. Most of these creatures were shipped to markets in cities large and small, where a buffalo tongue or a goose would sell for a few pennies.

The fate of the passenger pigeon perhaps best illustrates how unrestrained exploitation destroyed American wildlife. During the early nineteenth century, the passenger pigeon most likely accounted for half of all the birds in North America. An unusually large flock observed at Fort Mississisaugua, Ontario, in the early 1800s tallied an estimated 3.7 billion birds. Sport hunter William Leffingwell, in a memoir that appeared as a chapter of an 1890 book titled *Shooting on Upland, Marsh, and Stream,* wrote, "The immensity of some of these flocks of pigeons almost surpasses belief, and it is well for those of us who have seen and enjoyed these sights that there are living witnesses to substantiate what we say."

Naturally, these immense numbers could not escape the notice of anyone with a gun, net, club, or an inclination to slaughter. One of the largest roosts on record occurred in 1878, near Petoskey, Michigan, where it remained from March until August. Covering about 250 square miles, it immediately drew the attention of four hundred to five hundred of the estimated five thousand hunters thought to make a living from pigeons at that time. Local Indians and white residents also converged on the flock, both for sport and for commerce. Hunters raked the trees with shotgun fire, knocked nests to the ground with clubs, and netted adult birds. Boys cut down trees to get at nests, wringing the necks of baby birds. In all, according to observers, at least 1.5 million passenger pigeons were killed at Petoskey.

At the start of the nineteenth century, North America's passenger pigeon population had stood at about six billion birds, but even this number could not withstand both the heavy hunting and the loss of woodland habitat. The pigeons were hunted incessantly until 1896, when the last big flock—a relatively paltry 250,000 birds—settled at Bowling Green, Ohio. As always, hunters converged. In the end, only about 5,000 pigeons escaped, disappearing over the horizon and vanishing into history, for never again was a large flock of passenger pigeons seen winging its way across the sky. The species did not show up again until March 24, 1900, when one lone passenger pigeon arrived in Pike County, Ohio, and was promptly killed by a young boy. As the last wild passenger pigeon on record, the bird died not far from the site along the Ohio River where, eighty-seven years earlier, naturalist and artist John James Audubon had observed what he estimated to be one billion pigeons passing overhead.

The unrestrained hunting that led to the extinction of the passenger pigeon also devastated many other species of bird and animal. A few, including the Carolina paroquet, a bright green and yellow parrot-like species that ranged across much of the Southern woodland, became extinct. By the close of the nineteenth century, many nature enthusiasts believed that a host of other species would soon vanish as well. In response to the plight of wildlife and the unremitting slaughter, the conservation movement was born.

The natural world in the United States reached this low ebb because until the end of the nineteenth century few people cared whether wild things survived or perished, and those who did were not certain how to address their concerns.

During the years of settlement, wilderness and nature were seen as antiprogress and even, in an avowedly Christian nation, anti-Christian. Early ministers, such as the witch-slaying, New England Puritan Cotton Mather, used nature in their sermons as a metaphor for hell and ungodliness. The settlers were portrayed as the messengers of God, bringing to the New World the holiness of order, cleaning up unruly forests, replacing wild beasts with livestock, and dispossessing the native peoples, whom many believed were probably soulless anyway. The most pointed expression of the settlers' orthodoxy was made in 1845 by John Louis O'Sullivan, who wrote in the *United States Magazine and Democratic Review:*

COPYRIGHTED
1903
BY
??S KINSEY.

Loggers rest on and around a huge tree felled in a Washington forest in 1905. As settlers swept westward across the nation, they turned forests into pasture and stubble. The ancient trees that remain in the Northern Pacific region represent a tiny percent of what was once northern North America's vast virgin forest.

"Our manifest destiny is to overspread the continent allotted by Providence for the free development of our yearly multiplying millions."

O'Sullivan was writing before the Industrial Revolution started to darken the atmosphere with its effluents, poisoning rivers and shores, and before humanity had the technological skills for denuding natural landscapes with ease. He had no real idea what his clarion call meant for the continent or the world. He lived in an optimistic age, when human development seemed neither to possess a limit nor to have need of one.

By the close of the nineteenth century, loggers had cut down most of the Eastern forests and were earnestly hacking down the last virgin forests in the Great Lakes region, massive old trees whose like has never been seen there again. Waste was rampant in the timber industry; millions of board feet were lost in the burning or trashing of small trees and in the inefficient processing of trees into lumber. One logging company, operating around the Great Lakes at the turn of the century, cut enough trees to produce one million board feet of lumber (a board foot is a foot square and an inch thick) but in fact made only 160,000, wasting more than 80 percent of the trees. In the arid Southwest, cattle and other livestock were entering grasslands in record numbers, eating and trampling the region into desert or near desert. Early in the 1870s, some five million cattle fed upon the Western grasslands; by the early 1890s, the number had swollen to twenty-five million.

Wetlands also came under assault. In the 1850s, Congress gave sixty-five million acres of wetland to the states, provided they agreed to drain them for development. The nation entered a period of drainage mania. By the end of the century, plans were under way to drain the largest wetland in the world, the Florida Everglades.

While most of the nation was busy congratulating itself on the course it was following, another observer was concluding that social and economic collapse was the only destiny that would manifestly follow unbridled development. This was George Perkins Marsh, a lawyer, historian, and diplomat, fluent in twenty languages. In 1864, Marsh published a book that marked the first overt expression of concern over what human development was doing to the natural world. In *Man and Nature*, Marsh contended that throughout history human development had degraded nature, harming human society as well as wilderness. He showed how misguided irrigation schemes that poisoned agricultural lands had led to the decline of ancient Middle Eastern cultures. He offered this as a warning to development-minded Americans, pointing out that land management, or the lack of it, was disturbing natural balances across the American landscape. As an example, he described how some streams in deforested areas of the eastern United States had stopped flowing because logging had altered the movement of water through the soil. He concluded that humankind was damaging the planet at some risk to its own survival.

Marsh's weighty discourse indicates that society, or at least a small portion of it, was beginning to think about humanity's responsibility to the globe. His thesis was grounded in pragmatism, in concern for the way nature's degradation would harm human life. And although a social movement was growing that focused on the idea of appreciating nature for its aesthetic value, the conservation movement that developed toward the end of the nineteenth century continued in this practical vein. Economic concerns underlay numerous early preservation efforts, many involving the creation of parks and forests. Yellowstone, the world's first national park, was created in 1872 as an outgrowth of an expedition funded by the railroad industry in the hope of finding lands that would make a suitable tourist destination. A model for this idea was Yosemite State (now National) Park in California, to which tourists were flocking via railroad. For decades, the railroads maintained a vested interest in the creation of national parks. Glacier National Park, designated thirty-eight years after Yellowstone, was primarily the work of railroad magnate Louis Hill, who knew a good tourist attraction when he saw one. People were increasingly interested in natural beauty, and business interests were happy to supply it to them.

Economics also played a critical role in other conservation developments. The federal government's first foray into

George Perkins Marsh was the first to voice a public warning that irresponsible development and wanton destruction of natural resources would endanger human survival. As evidence, he pointed to the experiences of ancient cultures and to modern indications that deforestation was killing streams in the eastern United States.

A consummate advocate for wilderness, John Muir was instrumental in winning or increasing protection for many natural areas, including national forests and Yosemite National Park. The founder of the Sierra Club, Muir once wrote that in a war between the beasts and mankind, he would be tempted to sympathize with the beasts.

wildlife protection was the Commission of Fish and Fisheries, created by Congress in 1871 to study the need for the protection of edible fish. In 1886, Congress created the Department of Agriculture's Division of Economic Ornithology and Mammalogy, the earliest ancestor of the U.S. Fish and Wildlife Service, to study how wild creatures affect agriculture.

The practical basis for protecting nature can perhaps best be seen in the federal government's first organized attempt at protecting large stretches of wild land. This was the early development of the National Forest System. The key players in this issue were John Muir and Gifford Pinchot.

Muir was born in Scotland in 1838 and moved to America as a child, when his father took up farming in Wisconsin. In 1862, Muir fled to Canada to avoid being drafted into the Civil War, a conflict whose violence he abhorred and to whose combatants he felt little allegiance.

In Canada he roamed the wilderness and acquired a spiritual affinity for nature. Returning to the United States in 1869, Muir lived in California's Yosemite Valley for four years, studying glaciers, forests, and wildlife. In 1874, he left the valley to marry a woman he had met in the San Francisco Bay area and settle on her family farm. He began writing popular articles for magazines such as *The Atlantic* and *Century*, quickly becoming a voice for wilderness protection. He spoke of a world in which humanity was not the center of the universe, but a part of it. "Nature's object in making animals and plants might possibly be first of all the happiness of each one of them, not the creation of all for the happiness of one," he wrote. "Why ought man to value himself as more than an infinitely small composing unit of the one great unit of creation? . . . The universe would be incomplete without man; but it would also be incomplete without the smallest transmicroscopic creature that dwells beyond our conceitful eyes and knowledge." More pointedly, in his 1916 autobiographical work, *A Thousand Mile Walk to the Gulf,* Muir wrote, "Well, I have precious little sympathy for the selfish propriety of civilized man, and if a war of races should occur between the wild beasts and Lord Man, I would be tempted to sympathize with the bears."

Muir's love of wilderness compelled him to join forces
with other nature enthusiasts in an effort to win protection
for the nation's forests, which the logging industry was rapidly depleting. He wrote a series of magazine articles in support
of forest preservation and helped persuade Congress to pass
the 1891 Forest Reserve Act, which authorized the president
to create national forests. The law was enacted out of a
widespread fear that the logging industry was laying waste
the nation's forests and creating conditions that would lead
to a timber famine. But although the law empowered the
president to create national forests, it did not provide any
guidance for forest protection. Muir believed that America's
forests, or what was left of them—he thought them already
badly diminished by logging—were a national treasure that
should be preserved for the pleasure and wonder of succeed-
ing generations of citizens. He pursued this goal on a local
level in California, where in 1892 some of his colleagues prevailed upon him to help establish a group that would work
for the preservation of parklands in the High Sierras. Thus
the Sierra Club was born, with Muir as its leader. The group
immediately set about winning stronger protection for
Yosemite National Park, Muir's old stomping ground.

Meanwhile, Muir also was at work urging Congress to
keep the national forests inviolate. In one of his many articles and books on the subject, he wrote that logging in the
forests would ultimately leave the United States as vacant of
trees as the Middle East or Spain, whose ancient forests had
been cut long ago. Only complete protection, he believed,
would spare the forests.

At the same time, an opposing camp was in the ascendant,
led by Gifford Pinchot, a wealthy Pennsylvanian who had
studied forestry in Europe. Pinchot believed, as did German
and French foresters, that forests should be protected not for
their own sake but as sources of lumber. He maintained that
cutting forests for lumber was no threat to the forests as long
as it was done under management plans that would, at least
in theory, allow the trees to regrow for further cutting. Forest
managers in Pinchot's day had not yet discovered that virgin
forests have many biological differences from the forests that
grow in previously cut areas. Pinchot won over Congress with

*Gifford Pinchot shared
the widespread belief
that forests should be
managed as a renew-
able source of lumber.
He helped persuade
Congress to open
national forests to log-
gers. As the first head
of the nation's new
Forest Service, he
institutionalized the
relationship, laying the
groundwork for one of
today's most bitter
battles.*

his ideas, and the national forests were opened to logging. This set the stage for today's battles over forest protection.

In 1905 Pinchot was named the first chief of a newly organized federal Forest Service, and he immediately set to work creating an organization designed to make national forests into timber reservoirs. While Pinchot's measures sought to avoid ruining the forests as sources of lumber, they did not emphasize the management of forests as wildlife habitats. In a sense, the conflict between Pinchot and Muir was a clash between two forms of pragmatism. Pinchot want-ed the forests saved primarily as sources of lumber, but also to prevent the destruction of streams caused by the erosion that follows clear-cutting along banks. Muir wanted the forests saved because he knew they supported wildlife resources valuable on several levels, including an aesthetic one. In the end, the less complex form of pragmatism—viewing the forest as a source of lumber—won out. Concern with the commercial value of wildlands would prevail throughout the early years of wilderness protection.

By the turn of the century the federal government was slowly making progress in the protection of wildlands—setting aside national parks, forests, and wildlife refuges—but it was play-ing a small to nonexistent role in the express protection of wildlife itself. In fact, some question existed as to whether or not the federal government could claim any legal authority over wildlife. The Constitution reserved management to the states, which were doing a poor job of enforcing the already permissive wildlife laws. Meat markets continued to consume populations of wild creatures. The fashion industry was push-ing species to extinction, as hunters in Florida slaughtered vast numbers of long-legged wading birds, such as ibises and egrets, so that the feathers could be used to trim women's garments.

It was the uncontrolled commercial hunting of birds that forced the federal government to become more actively involved in wildlife protection, and perhaps the individual most influential in creating that federal role was a man with an appropriate middle name, George Bird Grinnell.

Grinnell was a Yale graduate who in the 1870s explored

the Black Hills of Dakota as the staff zoologist for a cavalry expedition led by George Armstrong Custer. Grinnell was supposed to serve with Custer again on the Little Big Horn expedition, but work kept him from going. Spared a grim fate at Custer's Last Stand, Grinnell turned his love of the West into a powerful force for conservation, beginning in the late 1870s when he worked as a writer for one of the popular new fishing and hunting magazines, *Forest and Stream*.

By the mid-1880s, Grinnell had become the editor of *Forest and Stream*. This was a time of particular ferment for the conservation movement. Groups were being organized one after another for the protection of nature. Muir's Sierra Club was one. Another was the Boone and Crockett Club, a game protection group started by wealthy Eastern hunters, including Theodore Roosevelt, who feared they would soon have nothing to hunt. Grinnell earned his place in the conservation echelon with a February 1886 *Forest and Stream* editorial in which he declared, "We propose the formation of an association for the protection of wild birds and their eggs, which shall be called The Audubon Society."

The organization was named for John James Audubon, the man who, early in the century, had set out to paint life-size portraits of all North American bird species. After years in the field, he found a publisher for his work and went on to win international acclaim as an artist and naturalist. A childhood friend of the Audubon family, Grinnell had played with Audubon's children and knew the artist's widow well enough to call her Grandma.

The impetus for the Audubon Society was the slaughter of birds for the meat markets and for the millinery trade, which sometimes used entire birds to decorate women's hats. From colorful songbirds to American egrets, many species were threatened with extinction. In his editorial Grinnell wrote, "Very slowly the public are awakening to see that the fashion of wearing the feathers and skins of birds is abominable." The dwindling of birds, he wrote, particularly insect- and rodent-eating birds, represented a threat to farm crops. "The land which produced the painter-naturalist John James Audubon will not willingly see the beautiful forms he loved so well exterminated."

As editor of Field and Stream, *George Bird Grinnell in 1886 proposed formation of the Audubon Society. The group fought to protect wild birds, especially endangered songbirds and wading birds, which were being hunted for food and feathers.*

A wildlife artist and observer of nature, John James Audubon became the namesake for the Audubon Society and its magazine, first published in 1887 for a national membership of twenty thousand. The publication was dedicated to the protection of those birds "not used for food."

Public response was tremendous. By June 1886 the society, funded by *Forest and Stream*, had ten thousand members. By the end of the year, it had twenty thousand. In February 1887 the first issue of *Audubon* magazine rolled from the presses. It included articles on John James Audubon, the Baltimore oriole, and the fashion industry. The last was titled "Woman's Heartlessness." A short item noted the extinction of the quagga, a zebra-like African animal. The purpose of the magazine, an editorial avowed, was to "spread the Audubon movement as widely as possible, and in every way to foster its growth."

Growth was indeed fostered, so much so that the organization fell apart. By December 1888 the society, boasting fifty thousand members, was on the verge of collapse because the *Forest and Stream* staff could not keep up with Audubon Society demands, and the company could not afford to bankroll the burgeoning group. Although Grinnell had to disband the society, concerned individuals were undaunted. By 1896, local Audubon Societies were being formed across the nation. By 1900, they had been established in nineteen states, and in 1905 they banded together to form the group known today as the National Audubon Society. One of the society's goals was passage of a federal law protecting migratory birds.

The need for strong federal protection was underscored by

weaknesses in the first federal law designed to stem market hunting. This was the Lacey Act of 1900, which not only prohibited the interstate transportation of wild animals killed in violation of state law, but also allowed states to ban the importation of game killed legally in other states. The federal government was on safe constitutional ground with this law because the Constitution gives the government the power to regulate interstate commerce. Unfortunately for wildlife conservationists, the states were not interested in enforcing the act. To remedy this, Pennsylvania representative George Shiras III introduced a bill in 1904 that would place migratory birds under federal protection. Theodore Roosevelt, then president, supported it, but the law failed in Congress on the grounds that it was unconstitutional. A different bird protection law was finally enacted in 1913, but attempts to enforce it stalled in the courts, when its constitutionality was again brought into question.

Sensing that a new law would not make it through the courts, bird-protection advocates took a circuitous legal route. The courts had long recognized that federal treaties with other nations superseded state law. So in 1916 the Department of State signed a treaty with Great Britain, acting in Canada's behalf, calling for the protection of birds that migrated across the U.S.-Canadian border. Two years later, Congress passed the Migratory Bird Treaty Act, which implemented the treaty and gave federal agencies the authority to work for bird protection by instituting measures such as closed seasons on hunting. When the law was tested in the Supreme Court, the justices found it constitutional.

This marked the beginning of federal wildlife protection. In subsequent decades, federal protection of wild species and wild places became increasingly refined. Congress created the National Park Service in 1916 to administer the growing federal park system, which until then had been managed by the military. During the 1920s and 1930s, the need to protect waterfowl populations hard hit by drought led to expansion of the National Wildlife Refuge System and to improved refuge funding mechanisms. The National Forest System also expanded early in the century as the federal government sought to protect the timber supply and the integrity of waterways, which could be damaged by uncontrolled logging. Beginning in the 1940s, wildlife protection gained importance, leading, in the 1960s and 1970s, to such laws as the Endangered Species Act and the Marine Mammal Protection Act, which protects seals, sea lions, polar bears, whales, and other ocean mammals. A movement begun in the 1930s to win protection for wilderness areas on public lands led to passage of the Wilderness Act in 1964. This act seeks to protect the nation's most pristine areas from development and permanent human intrusion.

Today the protection of wild places and wild species has become an integral part of our society. The processes set in motion by early conservationists have brought many rewards. Species that Grinnell, and others like him, thought doomed to extinction—such as deer, bison, pronghorn, and wild turkeys—have proliferated again, reaching relatively large and stable numbers. Careful monitoring of species still at risk, including wolves, grizzly bears, and waterfowl, has replaced their willful slaughter and has helped some species to recover from the threat of extinction.

Many of the conservation groups that started late in the nineteenth century have gone the way of the quagga. The National Audubon Society is typical of those that survived. Begun with a narrowly defined purpose, the society gradually broadened its activities to include a vast range of issues, such as habitat protection, energy efficiency, population growth, air and water pollution, and farmland management. Today several hundred local and national conservation groups are working daily to protect wildlife, wilderness, and the health and integrity of the human environment. These organizations stand as monuments not only to the people who created them, but also to the thousands of people who have supported the groups through the years with funds and hard work. The present conservation and environmental community, through its educational programs and its activities in legislative halls, helps to shape federal and local policy on all ecological issues, from clean air to the protection of wildlands and endangered species, giving citizens a powerful voice in setting national policy.

Chapter Two

ENDANGERED SPECIES

Although many species seemed poised to vanish beneath the onslaught of hunting in the early years of conservation, hunting today is largely controlled, particularly in the developed world, and animal populations are monitored to help ensure that they do not decline. While some animal rights groups oppose hunting because they find it inhumane, most mainstream environmental organizations recognize that hunting, if properly managed, poses no biological threat to species that are not endangered.

Nevertheless, because of habitat destruction, more species are currently faced with imminent extinction than at any other time since dinosaurs disappeared from the Earth eighty million years ago. Within the next few decades the planet could lose half of all its living species—somewhere between five million and thirty million different types of plants and animals.

The wide range of these estimates shows how uncertain biologists remain about the number of species that exist. Surveys conducted in oceans and tropical rain forests consistently turn up new species, suggesting that the planet harbors far more unknown plants and animals than taxonomists (who classify living things) thought possible. But more important than the specific number of species that exist is the unprecedented rate at which they are being lost. As species sink into extinction, the biological communities they compose begin to collapse, like a wall with too many bricks pulled from it.

Since time immemorial, people have thought of nature as chaos and human civilization as order. In fact, nature is orderly. Relationships among species create a superstructure of mutually dependent living things. Only recently have experts gathered enough data to realize that removing individual parts can throw the whole of nature into chaos.

An adult female bald eagle recuperates from a bullet wound at a Canadian rehabilitation center. Most species of raptors have made a comeback since the insecticide DDT was banned in 1972, but many still suffer from reproductive failures and birth defects that have been traced to PCBs and other toxins. (facing page)

Flowers, which often rely on animals for pollination, pro-vide excellent illustrations of the interdependence found in nature. Many orchids, which represent the extreme in adap-tations to pollinators, are pollinated by male orchid bees that seek not nectar but floral fragrances, which the bees store in pockets on their hind legs. The fragrances attract a limited number of orchid bees, which fly from blossom to blossom collecting various fragrances. When an individual male bee obtains the right combination of scents, it suddenly becomes extremely attractive to other males, which swarm around it. The buzzing swarms of males in turn attract females, some-thing a lone male cannot do. If orchids were to vanish, the bees for which the flowers provide fragrance would disappear as well. Since the bees probably pollinate other plants, and both doubtless are food for other species, the orchids play a significant role in the survival of their ecosystem.

Less elegant but equally important interdependencies also underlie the survival of other species. The African elephant, by tearing down trees as it feeds, keeps plains regions open, a benefit to many other grassland species. Ironically, the ele-phants also help the trees they tear down to regrow, because seeds from species such as the acacia tree grow better if they have passed through an elephant. In addition, during times of drought elephants dig holes in riverbeds, creating pools of water useful to a wide variety of thirsty animals. Animals that support their ecosystem in such ways are called keystone species. If a keystone species vanishes, many other species may go with it.

Although plants and animals engage in highly complex interactions, species are only the building blocks of much larger biological communities. These communities, called ecosystems, are defined by their particular plants, animals, climate, soils, and other elements. Some plants and animals are uniquely adapted to life within only one type of ecosys-tem, while others can survive in a wide range of environ-ments. But in each case, species are confined by their evolu-tionary adaptations to life within certain limits.

The kangaroo rat, for example, is a nocturnal rodent of dry North American grasslands and deserts. Its large eyes help it to see in darkness. Its long hind legs enable it to jump

A bull elephant in Kenya tests his strength against a thorny acacia tree. Adult elephants eat more than seven hundred pounds of food a day. To satisfy this voracious appetite, elephants will knock down trees, thus helping to maintain open grasslands.

away from enemies; its long tail helps it keep its balance, as do its small, lightweight front legs, which can be withdrawn for streamlining. Even the rat's long whiskers help the animal to move rapidly, for as it runs it repeatedly touches the ground with its whiskers, apparently using them to find its way in the dark. The kangaroo rat feeds on grass seeds provided by native wild plants. Because the seeds are small, the rat does not require a powerful bite, so its jaw muscles are relatively weak for a rodent its size. The rat can go its entire life without drinking water. This alone requires many adaptations for the digestion of food and the metabolism of water.

The kangaroo rat is beautifully adapted to life in the desert. It survives where rodents native to forests or marshes would soon die. But taken from its natural habitat and put in a forest of the Pacific Northwest—where annual rainfall can be measured in feet, the forest floor is dense with rich, moist undergrowth, and trees shower the ground with nourishing but hard-shelled seeds—the kangaroo rat would die. It is tied to its habitat, the grassland ecosystem, by inescapable bonds.

Specialized animals such as the Australian koala bear, which subsists entirely on eucalyptus leaves, are usually limited to one habitat or very few. Generalized species, such as coyotes, wolves, and humans, can survive under a huge range of conditions. Coyotes are found in mountains, grasslands, deserts, even cities. Wolves once ranged from above the Arctic Circle south to the tropical zones of both hemispheres. Humans outperform both, but our adaptation is less physiological than behavioral. We shape our environment to our needs or re-create tiny pieces of friendly environment in hostile places—with enclosed shelters and temperature control, we can survive the bitterest cold and most intense heat. We have even invented submarines that serve as terrestrial cocoons in deep aquatic environments. Of course, in habitats of extreme hostility we can survive only briefly without support (food, water, oxygen) from our natural habitats.

The intimate link between a living plant or animal and its habitat suggests that no species—however hardy, intelligent, adaptable, or well-armed—can survive long if its habitat becomes so severely altered that the habitat no longer offers at least minimal levels of food, water, air, and shelter—if, in short, the habitat becomes uninhabitable. Because humankind has been appropriating large portions of the planet, especially in recent decades, for its own use, habitat loss has become the number one cause of species extinction.

This is not an academic matter of no consequence to the "real" world. The loss of species has serious ramifications for humanity and economics. If we remove enough plant and animal species, ecosystems will collapse. Since we, inescapably, also depend upon those ecosystems for various resources, ecosystem destruction will eventually impoverish our lives. For example, the foundation of our agricultural and medicinal industries—and of many other industries, from textiles to furniture to paint—is linked to wild species. The most obvious examples are toxic chemicals that kill birds and other wildlife but also threaten human health. Every species that declines, every species that becomes endangered, tolls a warning to us that something in the habitat is amiss, something is eroding the life-support systems, and something is threatening our very survival.

Species that become endangered tend to be the most vulnerable, most specialized, of a given ecosystem. These species, the most sensitively attuned to the state of their habitat, are the first to fall when the habitat degrades. Thus, they provide an early warning, to those who are listening, of possibly life-threatening changes.

In this manner, recovery of an endangered species does more than preserve an ecosystem's full complement of inhabitants. Because the habitat must be healthy enough for the species to survive, the protection and recovery of an endangered species also help to ensure the protection and recovery of its habitat.

The Endangered Species Act requires the federal government to recover listed species and to protect their habitat. This protection has had far-reaching effects, making the act one of the most important, and controversial, wildlife protection laws in the world.

The history of federal legislation for the protection of plants and animals facing extinction shows the circuitous route much wildlife law follows before it finally takes effect.

Congress first turned its attention to vanishing species in 1966, with the passage of the Endangered Species Preservation Act. This law authorized the secretary of the interior to compile a list of species that appeared to be in danger of extinction and susequently acquire lands for their protection. However, the law was ineffective because it did not restrict the taking of listed species or their use in commerce, and it offered few specific methods of habitat protection. In addition, it addressed only U.S. species, ignoring those in other nations.

This first law was followed in 1969 by the Endangered Species Conservation Act, which broadened the habitat protection measures of the original law and provided more funding for habitat acquisition. The new law also corrected a shortcoming of the first law, which called for the protection of endangered fish and wildlife but did not define the creatures covered by those terms. The 1969 legislation declared that protected animals were to include wild mammals, fish, birds, amphibians, reptiles, mollusks, and crustaceans. The new law also authorized the secretary of the interior to create a list of endangered species from other nations, to prohibit their importation, and to work with other nations for their preservation. The law directed the secretary of the interior and the secretary of state to convene an international meeting for creation of a global treaty on endangered species conservation.

This last measure has proved particularly successful. The Convention on International Trade in Endangered Species of Fauna and Flora was created at a 1973 meeting in Washington, D.C. Usually called the CITES treaty, or just CITES, the convention has been signed by more than one hundred nations and seeks to protect vanishing species from overexploitation in commercial trade. Under CITES, species jeopardized by trade are categorized into groups with differing levels of protection, based upon the severity of the situation.

Nations participating in the treaty can nominate candidates for listing. During biennial meetings, all CITES members vote on the candidates. For example, in the late 1980s the African elephant was so severely poached for ivory that it appeared to be racing toward extinction. Kenya and Tanzania asked that the elephant be completely excluded from trade. After it was, the ivory market collapsed and poaching nearly ceased; now elephant populations have begun to show signs of recovery.

CITES is subject to severe limitations, not the least of which is that it can impose no penalties on nations that ignore its restrictions. But with its acceptance in many countries, the treaty has been effective in the recovery of several species, including leopards and jaguars, once depleted by the fur trade.

In 1973, as CITES got under way, Congress was taking action on the national front, where it was clear that the current endangered species laws were not strong enough to recover most vanishing species. As Michael Bean explains in *The Evolution of National Wildlife Law,* even the 1969 act was undermined by its lack of a prohibition against the taking of listed species, its weak protections for endangered species' habitats, and its failure to offer protection to plants, insects, and many other species.

To remedy this, Congress passed the Endangered Species Act of 1973, and it is this law, much amended, that protects the nation's endangered species today. The law demands the conservation of habitats upon which endangered species depend and requires that all federal agencies protect and conserve listed plant and animal species and attempt to bring their populations to levels suitable for removing them from the list. It also defines wildlife and plant species as any member of the animal or plant kingdom.

For a species to be protected under this act, it must first be nominated by an individual or organization as endangered or threatened. "Endangered" means the species is likely to become extinct if unprotected. "Threatened" means it is likely to become endangered if unprotected. After nomination, the federal government determines whether the candidate species should be listed. If the candidate is a marine species, the National Marine Fisheries Service (NMFS) makes this determination. All other species fall under the jurisdiction of the U.S. Fish and Wildlife Service (FWS). The listing process, involving a review of scientific data, is supposed to take no longer than one year. If the candidate is listed, the appropriate agency designates its critical habitat— the area the species requires for survival—and creates a recovery plan that explains how the species will be protected and managed in order to return it to a population level at which it can safely be delisted.

Once a species is listed, it is protected from "take," which the law defines as harassment, harm, pursuit, hunting, shooting, wounding, killing, trapping, capturing, collecting, or attempting to do any of these. Take also includes destruction of the species' habitat, since loss of habitat almost always results in at least the threat of harm. Additionally, the law forbids any federal funding of projects that will harm a listed species.

To determine whether a project will do harm to listed plants and animals, the FWS and the NMFS engage in a consulting process during which the proposed project is carefully investigated. If it is determined that the project may threaten a listed species, a "jeopardy decision" is issued. A 1992 study by the World Wildlife Fund showed that of some seventy-five thousand federal projects subject to consultation between 1987 and 1992, only nineteen were blocked or terminated by the act. Usually, if a jeopardy decision results, projects are not canceled but modified to accommodate the listed species. A National Wildlife Federation study of jeopardy decisions issued between 1979 and 1986 found that only 1 percent of the projects were canceled.

In theory, the Endangered Species Act protects all listed species from harm or trade and protects their critical habitat as well. But between enactment and implementation of the law lie many obstacles, including Congress, industry, and agriculture. When we examine the fates of the wolf, grizzly bear, California condor, and black-footed ferret, it becomes apparent how these forces come into play.

The gray wolf once ranged freely throughout most of North America. Ernest Thompson Seton, a naturalist whose fictional stories about wildlife were best-sellers early in the century, estimated that before European settlement, North America was home to two million wolves. Although the figure is a crude assessment, any species that covered most of the continent and was common into the nineteenth century was certainly numerous.

Hunting, habitat loss, and predator control programs—both private and governmental—reduced wolf numbers in the lower forty-eight states practically to zero by the 1930s. Today, only about twelve hundred gray wolves survive south of the Canadian border, and except for a handful in Michigan and Montana, all inhabit northern Minnesota.

It is difficult to assess how protection under the Endangered Species Act has affected the gray wolf. Listing the wolf brought an end to a Minnesota wolf-hunting season, a restriction that may have helped to stabilize the state's population. Listing also led to the creation of a federal program for removing wolves that prey upon livestock, thus reducing the farmers' need to kill the wolves.

But despite these measures, listing seems to have had little effect on wolves. Their numbers in the lower forty-eight states have only remained stable, rather than increasing significantly, and the animal's range has scarcely expanded. Where expansion has occurred—in Montana and Idaho along the Canadian border—it has been accomplished not by government planning but by the random movements of a dozen or so Canadian wolves that, since the early 1980s, have wandered in and out of the United States and bred south of the border. Whether the law has offered useful protection to these animals is uncertain because Western ranchers, convinced that wolves prey on livestock, surreptitiously kill and dispose of wolves, a practice referred to as "shoot, shovel, and shut up." Additionally, during the first fifteen years of the Endangered Species Act, almost all federal efforts in behalf of the wolf were reactive rather than proactive.

The late 1980s, however, yielded notable progress in federal wolf management. One example concerns the red wolf, a species that once ranged throughout the Southeast, particularly in swampy areas. Smaller than the gray wolf, it fed on rabbits and other small animals. Habitat loss, crossbreeding with coyotes, and hunting nearly wiped it out. In 1973 the Fish and Wildlife Service captured all remaining wild red wolves, about seventeen animals in bad condition due to disease and parasites. These animals bred in captivity, and in 1987 the FWS began releasing red wolves into the Alligator River National Wildlife Refuge in North Carolina. Subsequent releases were made in 1988 on Bull Island in South Carolina's Cape Romain National Wildlife Refuge. More than two hundred red wolves now survive in captivity, and approximately thirty red wolves are doing well in the wild.

More ambitious plans for the reintroduction of gray wolves into parts of the West have met with heavy opposition from the ranching community. In the 1980s, ranchers seemed likely to win the fight, especially given the Reagan and Bush administrations' lackluster support of the endan-

A Mexican gray wolf takes to the high ground of its enclosure in Albuquerque, New Mexico. The subspecies once ranged across Mexico, Texas, Arizona and New Mexico, but now exists only in captivity. Offspring from about two dozen wolves will be released by the U.S. Fish and Wildlife Service into the wild, if an acceptable location can ever be found.

gered species program. However, the mood of the nation is changing as citizens show a growing interest in their wildlife heritage, and this mood is compelling the Fish and Wildlife Service to move ahead with reintroduction plans for the gray wolf.

One proposed reintroduction site is Yellowstone National Park, where the wolf was wiped out in the 1930s by federal control programs, ostensibly for the protection of deer, elk, and other game animals. A survey conducted during the late 1980s in Yellowstone by Defenders of Wildlife, an environmental group headquartered in Washington, D.C., showed that park visitors overwhelmingly favored restoration of the wolf to Yellowstone. The wolf is the only large mammal originally found in the park that is not still there. Reintroducing it will help right the natural balances of the ecosystem and may help control the proliferation of elk, which tend to overpopulate.

The Fish and Wildlife Service also is attempting to reintroduce the Mexican gray wolf, a Southwestern subspecies that is extinct in the wild, to parts of its former range. The FWS has been breeding the wolves in captivity since about 1980 and has formulated plans for releasing them in parts of Arizona and New Mexico. A leading potential reintroduction site is the federal White Sands missile range in southeastern New Mexico. A military base, the area is not open to the public and contains a large deer population that could provide food for the wolves. But local ranchers have stifled the plan, fearing wolves will leave the missile range and prey on their cattle.

Experience in northern Minnesota farm country, where far more wolves roam than the FWS will ever restore to any area, suggests that wolves represent little threat to livestock. Some twelve thousand farms lie in the wolf's Minnesota range, but only forty report livestock losses in an average year. The yearly average loss of livestock to wolves is about five head of cattle and twelve sheep for every ten thousand animals grazed in the area.

Despite federal plans to remove troublesome wolves from reintroduction sites and to compensate ranchers for lost livestock, western ranchers have continued to oppose wolf

restoration. Similar opposition, and some bureaucratic blun-
dering, have limited the recovery of another predator, the
grizzly bear.

The largest predator south of the Canadian border, the grizzly once ranged throughout the West, with occasional excur-
sions east across the Mississippi. When Lewis and Clark,
familiar with the smaller and more docile Eastern black bear,
went West in 1804, they were shocked by the ferocity of the
Great Plains grizzlies. This aggressiveness contributed to the
species' doom, for ranchers wanted no part of such a beast,
capable of bringing down a full-grown bull with a single
blow of its paw. The grizzly, once perhaps 50,000 to 100,000
strong in the West, today numbers only about 1,000 south of
the Canadian border. Most of those animals are found in
Glacier National Park, which shares the population with
Canada.

The grizzly joined the gray wolf on the earliest endangered
species list. Though its numbers were extremely low, it was
listed not as endangered but as threatened, because this
offered more latitude for removal of bears if they jeopardized
livestock. As with the wolf, biological interests were pushed
aside by politically powerful commercial interests, even
though the grizzly survives almost entirely in national parks
and national forests. To avoid conflicts with ranchers who
lease grazing lands in national forests and on other public
lands, the Fish and Wildlife Service delayed designating
critical habitats for the grizzly. No areas were set aside until
the 1980s, when seven sites in the Northwest were selected
as recovery zones.

While the grizzly has had to do without special protection
offered by habitat designation, it has had some bastions.
Yellowstone and Glacier national parks, the grizzly's last two
major stretches of occupied habitat in the lower forty-eight
states, are closed to hunting, grazing, and other consumptive
activities such as mining and logging. Nevertheless, in 1969,
a particularly controversial event involving grizzly management occurred in Yellowstone National Park: The National
Park Service decided that park grizzlies and black bears had
become too dependent upon food obtained from park dumps.

After feasting on salmon, a grizzly sow leads her cubs away from the stream. Alaskan grizzlies are not endangered, but their relatives in the lower forty-eight states are in trouble. Recently increased protections mandated by the Endangered Species Act have given biologists hope for the bears' recovery.

The Park Service shut down the garbage dumps. Although two researchers who had studied Yellowstone's grizzlies for a decade, John and Frank Craighead, warned that most of the park's bears were garbage-dependent, park authorities persisted in believing that a large number of grizzlies still roamed the back country, independent of people. After closing the dumps, the park service began to kill grizzlies that approached people or raided garbage bins in nearby towns. As a result, the Yellowstone grizzly population reached an all-time low, probably fewer than two hundred bears.

The number remained low into the early 1980s. Surveys indicated that the population was 30 percent below the minimum recommended by the federal grizzly recovery plan. Only about one quarter of the animals were females. Because grizzlies breed slowly, biologists feared the population would never reach the three hundred called for in the recovery plan, especially since poachers and park authorities were still killing an average of three or four bears yearly.

In 1982, Roland Wauer, chairman of the Interagency Grizzly Bear Steering Committee, which monitored grizzly recovery efforts, wrote to committee members: "Evidence persists that the population of grizzly bears within the greater Yellowstone ecosystem has seriously declined in recent years. Unless some change occurs to reduce the grizzly's mortality rate soon, the probability of retaining this wildland species in Yellowstone National Park is minimal."

This warning did not go unheeded. The 1980s saw a revitalization of grizzly protection. A large threat to the grizzly was removed when the Forest Service ruled that ranchers who grazed livestock on national forest land would be required to move their herds if a grizzly appeared in the vicinity. Previously, ranchers had been permitted to kill bears they perceived as a threat to their stock. In addition, the agencies involved in grizzly recovery undertook educational programs that taught residents and visitors how to bear-proof campsites and Dumpsters. This reduced the number of animals that had to be removed. The agencies also changed the grizzly recovery plan to limit human-caused bear deaths—the primary source of grizzly mortality—to no more than two females yearly during any six-year period. This would protect against excessive removals, since even problem bears would not be killed after the limit was reached.

Another trouble spot for grizzlies in recent years lay in northwestern Montana. Though the bear was listed as threatened, the state allowed an annual open hunting season. Hunting threatened species is permitted only if a population is so large that it jeopardizes its own survival. Since Montana had no data to support its claim that the bear population should be hunted, environmental groups questioned the legality of the hunting season, and Defenders of Wildlife sued to stop the hunt until sufficient data were collected. This brought grizzly hunting to a halt in Montana in the late 1980s.

Now that the federal agencies involved in grizzly recovery have begun taking their task more seriously, the grizzly has shown signs of recovery. Its numbers in Yellowstone are closing in on the three hundred outlined by the grizzly recovery plan as the goal for delisting, and biologists believe every reason exists for optimism. The big problem for grizzlies in the lower forty-eight states is continued development on public lands outside the national parks. Although the grizzlies are limited largely to the parks, they do roam into nearby national forests and onto private lands, where they can run afoul of people engaged in logging, mining, and other activities. For grizzly conservation to succeed, means must be found to allow grizzlies to occupy habitats outside park lands without the threat of destruction.

The California condor has left its fossil remains in New York, Florida, Nevada, New Mexico, and Texas, a sign of how widely it ranged eleven thousand years ago. By the early nineteenth century its range had primarily shrunk to the West Coast, where it fed on the remains of whales, sea lions, and other large mammals.

The condor is a relic of an earlier time, when mammoths and woolly rhinos roamed North America. Paleontologists believe the condor—a type of vulture that is the largest bird in North America, with a wingspan reaching ten feet—was adapted to feeding on large mammal carcasses. Its range shrank as most big mammals became extinct after the most recent glaciation.

It is unlikely that more than one hundred condors survived into the twentieth century. Most disappeared as a result of habitat loss and hunting after European settlement. The species' numbers continued to dwindle until, in the 1980s, the entire population lived in the rugged forested valleys of Southern California, where the birds soared over mountains that looked down upon Los Angeles and the California freeway system. Although the bird appeared on the 1966 endangered species list, and the Fish and Wildlife Service produced a condor recovery plan in 1975, the species population did not rise above forty during the 1970s. In 1979, the FWS decided to radio-tag all surviving condors, marking them with devices that transmitted a radio signal by which biologists could track each bird. The FWS also reported that it would take birds into captivity for breeding.

Some conservation groups opposed both measures, fearing that the radio transmitters would interfere with the birds' behavior and that the captive birds would never be returned to the wild. Others argued that since the birds were dying off anyway, the measures could do no harm and might help. The National Audubon Society, which had for years worked with the FWS on condor recovery, backed the agency's plan. The California Fish and Game Commission subsequently gave the FWS permits for capturing condors. Captures, which began in the early 1980s, were halted briefly when a young bird died while researchers were handling it. This crisis came to an end when experimental work with Andean condors, a nonendangered species from South America, proved that birds reared in captivity could survive in the wild. In addition, researchers began taking eggs and hatching them in captivity.

By early 1984 the recovery plan seemed to be moving along smoothly; then, in March, the death of a five- or six-year old male condor led to a new burst of controversy. This loss of a mature male from a wild population thought to number only eleven birds was bad enough, but within the next thirteen months six more condors died. In December 1986, the Fish and Wildlife Service decided to capture all remaining condors.

This move was vehemently opposed by many conservation groups, including Audubon, for fear that once all the birds were captured the FWS would have no reason to protect condor habitat. Audubon staff also believed that birds reared in captivity, when released into the wild, would need wild birds as guides to the feeding and roosting sites. Society members also believed that the wild population was an essential backup in the event that something went awry with the captive birds. However, when it became clear that the wild birds were rapidly dying off for unknown reasons, Audubon relented. The last wild condor was captured on Easter Sunday 1987. This was a seven-year-old male, and he was added to the thirteen condors held at the San Diego Wild Animal Park. These and thirteen others held at the Los Angeles Zoo were the last of the California condors.

The zoo and the wild-animal park remained the sole captive-breeding sites for the condor until 1993, when the Peregrine Fund, a private conservation group that specializes in bird-of-prey conservation, built a condor breeding facility. By summer 1993, the condor recovery project was maintaining fifty-six living birds.

In October 1991, two condors bred in captivity, a young male and a young female, became the first to be released into the wild when they were set free in Los Padres National Forest, which lies within former condor range. The male died the following October after ingesting antifreeze. In December 1992, four more females and two males, aged six to eight months, were released into Los Padres. Two of these died as a result of accidents with power lines. The FWS is now attempting to shift the birds into more remote areas, where they will be less susceptible to human influence. Also being considered is a plan for releasing birds into a remote area north of the Grand Canyon. If this succeeds, it will quite likely be the first time that condor range has expanded in thousands of years.

The black-footed ferret is a weasel-like inhabitant of prairie dog towns, where it feeds on the very creatures that dig the burrows in which it lives. Before European settlement of the Plains, prairie dog towns covering several hundred square miles were not uncommon, and early travelers reported towns covering several thousand square miles. Farming destroyed the towns in some areas, and in others ranchers poisoned the prairie dogs. The ferrets themselves fell victim to the poisons, as well as to the loss of the prairie dogs, whose range became increasingly reduced. The result, for the ferret, was near extinction.

The black-footed ferret was probably never a very common animal. First reported by John James Audubon in 1851, the species vanished for the next quarter of a century. Naturalists of the era came to doubt that such a species existed. It was never well studied and remained obscure even as the expansion of ranching pushed it toward extinction. By the 1970s, scientists suspected that the creature had vanished.

Then, on September 26, 1981, a dog on the John Hogg ranch west of Meeteetse, Wyoming, came home with a dead animal in its jaws. The rancher, faced with the corpse of an animal he had never seen, took it to a taxidermist, who suspected it was a black-footed ferret. He turned it over to the state wildlife agency, which called in the Fish and Wildlife Service. Biologists soon visited the Meeteetse area, where

The weasel-like, black-footed ferret was nearly exterminated by a federal campaign to eradicate prairie dogs. Recovery efforts had brought the species back from the brink of extinction when disease reduced the population to just eighteen animals. Now, nearly ten years later, the ferret is again well on the road to recovery.

they found a ferret population centered on a white-tailed prairie dog town. The entire known range of the ferret population covered only sixty square miles. Biologists began studying the animals and keeping tabs on their numbers. In 1984, the population peaked at about 130 animals.

In 1985 the ferrets began dying off, victims of distemper. At least one biologist suspected that the researchers themselves had inadvertently brought the distemper virus into the prairie dog town, perhaps carried from someone's pet. The FWS eventually captured all the remaining ferrets that could be found, only eighteen animals.

As with the California condor, captive breeding has proved highly successful. Today black-footed ferrets are kept at the Wyoming Game and Fish Department's Sybille Wildlife Research Unit north of Laramie; at the National Zoo's Front Royal, Virginia, research center; and at the zoo in Omaha. The project has raised the captive population to about 310 animals. In 1991, the FWS released forty-nine young ferrets into a prairie dog town in Shirley Basin, Wyoming, the first ferrets to be returned to the wild. Since then, another 150 have been released in the basin. The project's goal is to establish ferrets in four to six Western states during the next ten years.

The histories of the wolf, grizzly bear, condor, and black-footed ferret make telling points. One is that species without protection tend to decline. The second is that, guided by the best available scientific knowledge, federal recovery plans can bring results that, biologically speaking, are spectacular. Yet the twenty-year history of the Endangered Species Act has seen only a handful of species delisted, including the Pacific gray whale, the American alligator, and some populations of brown pelican.

Results are slow, despite the hope offered by the condor and ferret programs, because most rare species take years to increase in number and to expand their ranges. Extraordinary endeavors, such as the captive-breeding programs, are expensive and could not feasibly be undertaken for the approximately nine hundred domestic species that are listed. For the most part, recovery actions include little more than protection of listed species in their natural habitat and scientific monitoring of their populations.

Even this modicum of support has often been missing. Various powerful industries have succeeded in winning congressional approval for amendments that diminish the protective potency of the Endangered Species Act. Moreover, under some presidential administrations, even the agencies in charge of endangered species management have stood in the way of protection and recovery simply by refusing to implement the law.

Black-tipped and other sharks are put on display at a Key West pier. Recreational catches of sharks off U.S. waters—some 22 million pounds a year—combined with a growing commercial take in the late 1980s led to regulations limiting the catch of these slow-breeding creatures.

An additional administrative problem lies in the sheer number of listed and candidate species. Not only do the Fish and Wildlife Service and the National Marine Fisheries Service lack the funding to develop recovery plans for all listed species, they also have a backlog of nearly four thousand candidates for listing. By the time all these decisions are made, many of the species will already be extinct. Unless funding and staffs are increased, the endangered species program, like George Bird Grinnell's original Audubon Society, may be crushed under the burden of its own administrative weight.

Even when protection for endangered species is enacted nationally, it is often undermined locally. For example, the main cause of sea turtle deaths off Florida is drowning in fishing trawl nets. The National Marine Fisheries Service designed and satisfactorily tested a device that would exclude sea turtles, an endangered species, from trawl nets, but many fishermen in Florida and along the Gulf Coast have resisted their use, arguing that the devices, which cost about five hundred dollars each, are too expensive. Some fishermen threatened to burn the boats of those who use the devices.

Counteracting the groups aligned against endangered species protection depends upon strong public support for implementation of the law. Public-opinion surveys show that Americans overwhelmingly favor wildlife protection and that those who thwart the Endangered Species Act tend to be powerful economic interests whose political clout is greater than their head count. To ensure that species are not lost, the public will have to express strong support for endangered species recovery.

Of course, the best protection is that which keeps species from becoming endangered in the first place. Unfortunately, the excesses of past generations have left many species in critical situations, and only costly forms of crisis management will save them. But many other species, while jeopardized by habitat loss or overexploitation, could be conserved at relatively little expense if action is taken before they decline to endangered or threatened levels. Sharks, long subject to virtually uncontrolled commerce and sport fishing, provide a good example. In recent years, the taking of sharks has burgeoned. Sport fishermen alone caught nearly one billion pounds per year of shark worldwide in the late 1980s; in U.S. waters, the yearly sport catch stood at about twenty-two million pounds. This take, which affected about two-thirds of all shark species, was a threat to shark survival, because most sharks breed slowly, and their populations tend to drop precipitately under heavy hunting.

In the late 1980s, the increased commercial take was a cause for serious concern among shark biologists, who lacked data for determining how the catch was affecting shark populations off the U.S. coast. But rather than wait for sharks to become so scarce that they had to be listed as endangered or threatened, NMFS in 1993 issued regulations limiting the shark catch. Taking such action before a species becomes endangered is much less costly than delaying action until the species is in crisis.

One bright light in the world of endangered species conservation was lit during the final days of the Bush administration. As a result of a lawsuit brought by Fund for Animals and other groups, the administration agreed to streamline the listing process, expediting decisions on some thirteen hundred candidates. The settlement also brought another important development. The Fish and Wildlife Service agreed that it would take a multispecies, ecosystem approach to protecting wildlife, rather than trying to do it one species at a time. In short, this places the focus on protecting an entire habitat and allows a single program to affect a wide variety of species. Since for most species the best protection is ecosystem protection, this approach offers fresh promise for a more effective Endangered Species Act. But this does not mean that conservationists can relax their vigilance. Increased scrutiny must now be placed upon our ecosystems and the ways in which they are continuing to change under human domination.

Chapter Three

GRASSLANDS

Long before high-tech agriculture or even the horse-drawn plow came to the Americas, the central region of what would become the United States was cloaked in deep grasses. In the eastern portions of the Midwest, prairies of tall-grass species—some taller than a man on horseback—dominated the terrain. Farther west, from roughly the 100th meridian to the Rockies, lay the short-grass plains, covering an area so dry that it was known during the era of settlement as the Great American Desert or the American Steppe.

Rich with life, these grasslands were home to vast herds of bison, elk, deer, pronghorn antelope, and other hoofed species, as well as the wolves, bears, and mountain lions that preyed upon them. Rodents, including prairie dogs, ground squirrels, and gophers, served as food for the smaller predators—foxes, coyotes, and badgers. Like the grasslands of Africa and Asia, the American Steppe produced more animals by weight per acre than any other ecosystem.

Today, farms and ranches dominate these grasslands, and the native wildlife has been forced to retreat. With the exception of the cougar, the larger species have all been reduced to about 1 percent of their presettlement numbers. The plow wiped out virtually all of the tall-grass prairies that once cloaked Indiana, Illinois, Iowa, eastern Nebraska, and the north- and south-central states. Today about 1 percent of the tall-grass prairies remain, surviving only in small plots. They have become so diminished that some of the best places to find native species are cemeteries and railroad rights-of-way, where crops have not replaced wild plants.

Because of arid conditions and less fertile soil, the short-grass plains have fared somewhat better than the tall-grass regions. Instead of crops, the plains that sprawl across the eleven Western states—beginning in the Northwest with Washington and Oregon and ending in the Southwest with

A bison in Yellowstone National Park wades through a slow-moving stream. These symbols of the grasslands were nearly hunted to extinction before conservation efforts stabilized their numbers. (facing page)

Arizona, New Mexico, and Texas—were used to feed livestock. Although this preserved stretches of native wild grasses, the condition of grasslands in the West is not as healthy
as it appears—in many areas, exotic grasses from places as
distant as Africa have taken over the range, planted by
ranchers who thought the exotics would produce more livestock fodder than would native species.

As a consequence of these changes, the animal now dominant on America's grasslands is an import from the Old
World—the cow. Its most numerous companion on the
plains is the sheep. Together these animals have wrought
havoc on the structure of the grasslands environment and
have come to stand at the heart of one of the nation's most
controversial ecological issues—the leasing to ranchers of
the public lands that lie across much of the West.

The largest administrator of western public grasslands is
the Bureau of Land Management, which is also the largest
federal land managing agency—it is in charge of some 270
million acres, about 12 percent of the entire United States
and nearly 60 percent of all federally managed lands.

The Bureau of Land Management is in many ways a product of the grazing issue. Concern over western grasslands
dates to the turn of the century, when much of the West was
settled under various homestead acts. These laws gave settlers limited amounts of public land—usually less than seven
hundred acres—provided they lived on and improved it.
Because of the dryness of the region, the only land worth
settling lay along rivers, and this was where the pioneers
sought to stake their claims. They used the surrounding public lands to graze their livestock. Because they did not own
most of this land, ranchers tended to put as many animals on
it as possible on the presumption that if their cattle did not
use it, their neighbors' livestock would. As New Mexico
rancher Bill Cunningham says: "In the old days, when I was
quite young, why we really fought numbers with numbers,
because we were competitive against one another. And the
way you handled that was, you ran more [livestock] than the
neighbor did."

The result was that the lands were critically overgrazed.
During particularly wet years, a burgeoning herd of cattle

might not harm the grassland. But when the alternating plains cycles reached a dry phase, available forage was reduced and livestock ate more grass than the ecosystem could replace. So, over the course of years, the range lands deteriorated.

When drought struck the West in the 1930s, Congress began to take notice of the situation. The ranchers had long fought against controls on their grazing, but by 1934 the damage was so extensive it could no longer be ignored. Colorado representative Edward I. Taylor introduced the Taylor Grazing Act, and Congress passed it. It authorized the secretary of the interior to create grazing districts that ranchers could use only after purchasing federal permits. The law also included guidelines on how much livestock could be grazed on each acre of land.

This might have helped the grasslands had Congress not then put the new federal Division of Grazing under the command of a rancher, who went on to create grazing advisory boards made up of five to twelve ranchers but only one wildlife expert. The ranchers blocked efforts to reduce grazing, and little actually changed. But the ranchers still rankled under the division's efforts to impose fees and other restrictive measures, so in 1946 Nevada senator Patrick McCarran, an ally of the livestock industry, shepherded through Congress a bill that combined the Division of Grazing with the General Land Office to create the Bureau of Land Management. The reason for this merger was that in the new and underfunded agency, it was believed that grazing control would be completely neglected.

The first sign of real change did not come until 1969, when Congress enacted the National Environmental Policy Act. This law required the federal government to conduct studies—called environmental impact statements—of all federal actions and legislation that significantly affect the quality of human life. As a result of subsequent court cases, the law, designed to reduce environmental and social damage as well as threats to the quality of human life from pollution and other causes, was extended to include the protection of wildlife. As a result, in the late 1970s a federal court required the Bureau of Land Management to complete

Cattle at a University of New Mexico research ranch are part of experiments to protect and improve grazed lands. Described by some critics as nothing more than hoofed locusts, these imports from the Old World are poorly adapted to life in the arid Southwest.

141 environmental impact studies on its various land management programs, including grazing.

Since that time, the bureau has paid increasing attention to the status of its lands. So have conservationists and so has Congress. Nevertheless, studies show that today, nearly sixty years after the passage of the Taylor Grazing Act, well over half of all bureau grazing lands remain in fair to poor condition.

The bureau is not alone in leasing land to ranchers. The Forest Service does it as well. Some 104 million of the National Forest System's 191 million acres are tied up in grazing allotments that allow nearly fifteen thousand ranchers to put some 2.5 million cattle, sheep, and horses on national forest lands.

In return for leasing the public lands, the bureau and the Forest Service receive an annual fee of less than two dollars for each animal unit month, or AUM, which is roughly the amount of grass a cow will eat in a month. Similar leases on private land run from eight to sixteen dollars, sometimes more. The difference between federal and private fees essentially amounts to a federal subsidy of public-land ranchers. A study by the General Accounting Office for Grazing showed that in 1986, grazing brought an income of $14.6 million to the federal government, yet $39 million was spent on management, and another $25 million was spent for the removal of predators, other animals, and additional miscellaneous expenses. Attempts to raise the fees have been stymied by politically powerful livestock interests.

Even with these bargain fees, a federal study showed that many public-lands ranchers barely make a living from their livestock efforts. These ranchers told government interviewers that they continue ranching because they like the lifestyle. But these ranchers, according to a report by the House Committee on Government Operations, use less than 10 percent of public-lands forage. The other 90 percent goes to corporate livestock operations owned by the likes of Getty Oil, Union Oil, the Vail Ski Corporation (which leases one million acres of public land in Oregon), and one J. P. Simlot, reportedly Idaho's richest man and largest grazing permittee.

Government figures indicate that all public-land ranchers

An aerial view of New Mexico's Rio Puerco shows the effect of overgrazing on highly erodible soil. The banks cut by the river are thirty feet high in some places.

combined raise less than 5 percent of the nation's beef, or about 2.5 of the estimated 77 pounds of beef the average American consumes every year. The rest is raised on private land. In return for this small amount of meat, public grasslands sustain widespread ecological damage, which the government will eventually have to pay to repair. An additional expense is the Department of Agriculture's Animal Damage Control Program, which seeks to kill animals such as coyotes and mountain lions that are offensive to the livestock industry. In an average year, the program may kill 80,000 coyotes, 10,000 black bears, 200 mountain lions, and 125,000 prairie dogs. These are the target species. But many nontarget species consume the poisons and are caught in the traps put out for the targets. These include species from weasels to warblers, eagles to skunks.

The slaughter of wildlife in the name of livestock protection is an old tradition—in the nineteenth and early twentieth century, government programs wiped out wolves and grizzlies in most states at the behest of ranchers. Ironically, studies show that killing coyotes in any given area tends to boost the number of pups born to survivors, temporarily inflating the population and destabilizing it with young, inexperienced animals. Because younger animals are more likely to kill livestock, predator control can actually increase livestock depredations.

Jim Fish, a Department of Defense engineer who started the Public Land Action Network to help change grazing management, describes the effect of predator control on the prairie ecosystem: "Starting with a natural, balanced ecosystem, you bring in these exotic domestic livestock—sheep and cattle—and they start eating the vegetation, competing with the large mammals. The large mammals start declining in numbers. And then the predators that used to feed on the large mammals start feeding on livestock. Animal Damage Control comes in and destroys the predators. And then you get the rodents. Jackrabbits. Prairie dogs start overpopulat-

ing. The [control agents] come in and poison the prairie dogs. And shoot jackrabbits. And then the predators have even less to feed on. And so they feed even more on livestock. So they do more predator control. And so it's a vicious spiral downward. Always wildlife at the expense of these exotic domestic livestock."

The mere presence of cattle can harm the delicate, dry grasslands characteristic of parts of the Southwest. Cattle tend to gather around water sources, such as streams. Their hooves pound streambanks into mud, and the streams become silted. Native fish that need clear streams die off. Streamside vegetation declines as banks erode. In 1975, the Bureau of Land Management found that livestock grazing

Many public-lands ranchers consider mountain lions, wolves, and other predators unwelcome varmints. To accommodate the ranchers, the U.S. Department of Agriculture has trapped, shot, poisoned, and otherwise killed millions of "target species" through the years. Expensive and ineffective in the long run, the program also has killed untold numbers of eagles, ferrets, and other non-target animals.

Through the years, the federal Animal Damage Control program has killed off millions of prairie dogs. Despite a multimillion-dollar annual budget, this decades-old campaign of destruction has failed to eliminate the prairie dog. It has, however, nearly exterminated the black-footed ferret.

had damaged 80 percent of the stream habitat on the bureau's Nevada lands. In 1988, the Arizona Department of Fish and Game reported that less than 3 percent of Arizona's original stream habitat remained intact, as did less than 10 percent of New Mexico's: These losses stemmed primarily from livestock grazing. This is hazardous for wildlife because so many species depend on stream habitats. For example, 69 of New Mexico's 94 threatened vertebrate species are linked to stream habitats. So are 81 of Arizona's 115 threatened vertebrate species. Arizona streams once provided habitat for 32 fish species. Five are now extinct, and 21 are listed as threatened or endangered or are likely to be listed soon.

Other clues to the effects of grazing on grasslands are turning up at the National Audubon Society's Appleton-Whittell Research Ranch, which lies sixty miles outside Tucson, among the steep hills and windswept flats of south-eastern Arizona, flanked on all sides by distant mountains—the Huachucas, Santa Ritas, Whetstones, and Canelo Hills. The ranch encompasses 3,200 acres of private land and 4,600 acres leased from the state, the U.S. Forest Service, and the federal Bureau of Land Management.

Since the late sixties, the livestock-free ranch has been host to scores of scientists and research projects, yielding valuable information on the effects of grazing. During cattle-rearing years, oaks disappeared from the high, north-facing slopes they had cloaked for millennia. The old trees died off without replacement because the cattle ate the seedlings. Similarly, cottonwoods, Arizona walnuts, ash trees, and sycamores disappeared from streamsides. Grasses on flatlands and hillsides were eaten to the ground, and rainfall, no longer detained by plants, rushed across the land and into streambeds, flooding rapidly downstream and leaving waterways dry much of the year. A century ago, many of those streams would have run year-round, rainfall slowly percolating into them from surrounding hills as it eased through soil laced with grass roots.

At the Research Ranch, the damage shows some signs of reversing itself. "Since livestock were removed in 1968, erosion gullies have healed, riparian trees have regenerated, and biodiversity has generally increased," says Gene Knoder, manager of the ranch until his retirement in 1993. After twenty-five years without grazing, oaks are spreading across hillsides. Two taller grass species, plains lovegrass and Arizona cottontop, are more abundant on the Research Ranch than on neighboring livestock ranches.

But not all tree species are rebounding. While oaks and cottonwoods have begun to recover, sycamores are still doing poorly. Although cattle generally do not eat sycamore seedlings, they nevertheless affect them indirectly. Sycamore seedlings sprout in sandy streambeds, but grazing-induced floodwaters uproot them annually. Solving this problem, Knoder says, will require the cooperation of the federal Bureau of Land Management and the U.S. Forest Service, which manage the lands that surround the headwaters of the ranch's streams. Until then, grazing practices on these public lands will continue to deplete the grasses needed for ground cover to prevent flooding.

The changes livestock removal has brought to the ranch are reflected in its bird life as well. While the species that live on the ranch are not entirely different from those found on grazed lands, studies indicate that grazing does determine which birds will most prosper. Researchers found that three kinds of sparrows—grasshopper, Cassin's, and Botteri's—that are sparse or rare throughout the West are very common on the ranch. They seem to prefer to live and feed in the native tall-grass species that flourish in the absence of livestock. On grazed lands, however, they are generally outnumbered by species better adapted to an open habitat.

Among these are the horned lark and the lark sparrow, which most birders think typical of southeastern Arizona. However, ornithologists who have studied bird populations at the Research Ranch have reached a surprising conclusion about these seemingly characteristic Arizona grassland species. Before the advent of livestock grazing, horned larks and lark sparrows in the San Pedro Valley probably resided mainly around recently burned areas, because they eschew thick grasses. If, as fossil records indicate, no large grazing animals roamed southeastern Arizona during the past few millennia, then until this century most of the region would have been more heavily covered with tall-grass species, and grasshopper, Cassin's, and Botteri's sparrows would have been among the most common. It is only in the wake of grazing that horned larks and lark sparrows have come into ascendance. Were today's grasses freed from bovine appetites, many presently common birds would be replaced by species that prefer taller grasses. But since widespread cattle removal is unlikely, the Research Ranch has become an important refuge for tall-grass birds.

Birds are not the only measure of difference between grazed and ungrazed lands in the San Pedro Valley. Researchers have found that rodents are more abundant on the Research Ranch than on neighboring cattle outfits. This is probably a reflection of a more nourishing array of grass species or a sign of better seed production. It suggests that grasses are dense enough to provide rodents with sufficient cover to escape in greater numbers from predators. It also indicates that predator populations on the Research Ranch ultimately will be healthier, because rodents are important foods for predators from falcons to foxes. To be certain of this, however, more research is required.

Dense grass as a shelter from predators is almost certainly a factor in the survival of the bunchgrass lizard, a grassland species found mainly in the mountain meadows of southeastern Arizona and southwestern New Mexico. Carl Bock, a biologist from the University of Colorado, surveyed neighboring cattle ranches and found that the lizard is ten times more abundant on the Audubon ranch, where grass cover is nearly double that of the grazed lands. A relatively slow-moving species, the bunchgrass lizard will fall readily to predators unless it has access to shelter such as dense grass provides. Bock and his colleagues suggest that the lizard's restriction to mountain meadows is "associated with chronic and ubiquitous grazing of lower-elevation perennial grass-lands." Before the arrival of livestock in southeastern Arizona, the bunchgrass lizard, like the three sparrow species discussed, was probably more widespread.

Additional research has turned up similar findings in occurrence for other species, suggesting that grazing has pro-found effects on grassland ecology. Montezuma quail were common breeding birds on the Audubon ranch, while scaled quail were among the most abundant breeding birds on grazed land. Cottonrats, harvest mice, and hispid pocket mice were common on the Research Ranch, while deer mice and kangaroo rats were the most common rodents on grazed ranches. These differences in species distribution indicate that grazing may be changing the availability of cover and food, altering humidity and localized temperatures, and changing the occurrence of dominant plant species and, therefore, the occurrence of animals adapted to certain types of plants. Future research should replace such speculation with fact.

Perhaps the most interesting known effect that grazing has on species distributions was found in grasshoppers. During a 1992 Audubon-sponsored grazing conference in Tucson, a rancher expressed disdain for grasshopper research by saying, "I'm not in the business of raising grasshoppers." But studies at the Appleton-Whittell ranch suggest that, whether in the business or not, ranchers are indeed raising bumper crops of grasshoppers. In the early 1980s, biologists discovered that in autumn, when grasshopper populations are at their annual peak, the insects are nearly four times more abundant on grazed land than on the Research Ranch. This is in marked contrast to the summer, when grasshopper populations, though lower overall, are nearly four times more abundant on the Research Ranch. The difference is based on the types of species that flourish during different seasons. Those most abundant in summer are rapidly-maturing, grass-eating species, more common on the Audubon ranch than on grazed lands because of the ranch's greater amounts of grass. Slower-maturing, herb-eating grasshoppers take over both the ranch and neighboring lands in the fall, but produce much greater numbers on the grazed lands, where they find more herbal fodder and less grass.

Much of what scientists are uncovering on the Research Ranch may prove valuable to the livestock industry. Ranching is more directly dependent upon natural forces and ecology than most other U.S. businesses and industries. Cattle, after all, require grass. If researchers at the Audubon ranch discover means for enhancing the growth of grasses, cattle growers may profit. In any event, the manifold relationships that researchers are discovering among grassland species continue to illustrate the complex dynamics of the Earth's ecology and the risks of tampering with its natural systems.

As research at the Audubon ranch shows, the combination of western public grasslands with livestock need not always have harmful results for the ecosystem. Studies by prairie ecologist Jerry Holechek, a New Mexico State University professor, indicate that reducing the grazing levels currently used on public lands by about a third allows grasses to recover more quickly than in ungrazed areas. One reason for this is that grazing removes dead plant matter that can inhibit new growth and spur insect infestations and diseases. "The land can be grazed without destroying it," says Holechek. "But at the same time, I think range people and ranchers need to understand that the amount of grazing the land can sustain is probably less than the pressure we presently have in a lot of these arid areas." Cutting back on grazing can help ranchers in the long run, because as the ecosystem recovers and more grass grows, ranchers can increase livestock numbers. According to Holechek, the key to successful grazing is to ensure that livestock remove no more than 30 percent of available forage.

Because of the political clout of the livestock industry and the profits at stake, the grazing issue will continue to remain controversial and divisive. Some rangeland activists, incensed at the public-lands ranchers' long resistance to change, are hardening their opposition. One activist in the Southwest says that if ranchers do not become more responsible soon, cattle will be shot. Another, viewing a stream heavily eroded by grazing, said simply: "Cattle are an unnatural disaster in this part of the country. . . . They cannot, in my opinion, be managed in ways that are commercially profitable without this being the result in areas that are especially sensitive."

Meanwhile, in Washington, the issue of grazing fees continues to be hotly debated. Secretary of the Interior Bruce Babbitt has issued regulations that will gradually raise grazing fees over the next five years. He is also creating new grazing advisory boards that better balance livestock representation with representation for other interests. However, his measure offers little promise for improving rangeland conditions, and some conservationists fear the ranching industry will continue to dominate grazing management, especially as some congressional members with ties to the ranching lobby threaten to overturn Babbitt's regulations.

Chapter Four

Forests

When the first European settlers landed on the eastern seaboard they found themselves face to face with a vast green wall of trees. The forest extended west to the Appalachian Mountains and beyond, even crossing the Mississippi River in some southern areas. Records left by early explorers and settlers tell of the variety of forests that existed. In some, dense undergrowth made passage among trees difficult or impossible. In others, such as parts of Pennsylvania, no undergrowth existed. The huge tree trunks rose a hundred feet or more straight into the air, their leafy crowns shrouding the ground in shadow so dark that undergrowth could not survive. Some European travelers, finding the darkness ominous, climbed to the tops of the low Eastern mountains in search of open glades and sunlight. But the view they found was not pleasing, for all they saw were more mountains cloaked in trees, from horizon to horizon, an endless green sea.

A stream cuts through ancient forests in Oregon's Willamette National Forest. The Pacific Northwest is the last bastion of pristine forests in the lower forty-eight states. (facing page)

Some settlers viewed the forests as an immense resource ready to be turned into profit, others saw them as wastelands that demanded clearing. Either way, the forests were going to be cut. England coveted the trees of New England, which were taller and straighter than anything offered by European forests. These trees could be made into masts for the giant ships that enabled England to dominate the seas.

Though early settlers possessed only muscle and determination to power their axes and saws, the forests fell rapidly. Within two centuries of the Pilgrims' arrival at Plymouth, Massachusetts, New Englanders had used an estimated 260 million cords of firewood. Wood was also sold for export. From 1771 to 1773, 250,000 New England trees were converted into fuel for Caribbean sugar mills.

After 1776, these trees were used increasingly for American products. It is hard to imagine now how critical wood was in that era. It was used for heating homes and powering industries, for building houses, offices, stores, and factories. Machines were made mostly of wood, as were ships and carriages. Highways and roads were paved with wood. Early train rails were made of wood, as were the bridges the trains crossed. Settlers rapidly cut the forests, and in some instances, simply burned them so that the land could be converted into farms.

By the late 1800s, most of the forests east of the Mississippi River had been wiped out. The animals that lived in them were sent into retreat, including mountain lions, wolves, black bears, deer, elk, and moose. Cutting also affected the natural workings of the woodlands. Streams that had run year-round before deforestation began drying up for at least part of each year because there were no longer trees and vegetation to hold water in the soil. Rain ran rapidly off the bared earth and rushed into the streams, leading to flash floods followed by dried streambeds.

Although resources were not a concern to the early pioneers, by the late 1800s it was clear that the once seemingly endless land was finite and that the forests were almost gone. This resulted in Congress hastily enacting the Forest Reserve Act in 1891, authorizing the president to create federally protected forests on public lands. Because the law did not define the purpose of the forests, political conflicts soon developed in which naturalists sought to have forests protected for their own sake, while foresters wanted them protected as sources of timber, and loggers in the West wanted all protections lifted. Congress entered the fray when it realized what it had done by passing the 1891 law—namely, bestowed upon the president the unilateral authority to carve up federal lands into protected units. Regretting its action, Congress soon concluded that the law needed clarification.

Congress appointed a group to examine the issue, and in 1897 passed the Forest Service Organic Administration Act, which stated that national forests must be preserved to fulfill three purposes: to protect the forests themselves, to protect rivers and streams, and to provide a perpetual source of timber. This was very much in line with the thinking of forester Gifford Pinchot, whose training in European forestry placed his focus on forests as sources of wood. In 1905, Theodore Roosevelt made him the first director of the Forest Service, which has emphasized the forest-felling aspect of its mandate ever since. As a result, the national forests, particularly in the coastal Pacific Northwest, the Northern Rockies, and southeast Alaska, have become political battlegrounds, with conservationists fighting the logging industry in an effort to spare the last of the nation's virgin forests from cutting.

While forests once again cover much of the United States—the East is shrouded in forest from New England to Florida's northern border and from the Appalachian Mountains to the Atlantic Coast—almost all of this is second-growth forest, the type that replaces virgin forests after they have been cut. Second-growth forests are no substitute for virgin or ancient forests, which are biologically more complex. It is the latter that are of special concern to conservationists. Ancient forests can be readily distinguished from second-growth forests because trees in the ancient forests are of mixed ages, ranging from young saplings to old giants several centuries old. The ground in these forests is generally blanketed with ferns and other shade-loving undergrowth, and is punctuated with fallen trees that are slowly filtering their nutrients back into the soil, a process that can take as long as five hundred years. Fallen trees lie across streams, creating pools of still water in which fish, insects, and other aquatic species can breed. Among the living trees are many standing dead trees called snags, which provide homes for birds and other animals that live in cavities. In contrast, trees in second-growth forests are generally uniform in size because they are even-aged, meaning they started growing at the same time. Fewer snags occur, and the forest floor may be free of dead and rotting trees that give nutrients and life to the forest.

About 10 percent of the original forests of the Pacific Northwest remain uncut. Those that still exist are, for the most part, not the best forests the region once produced. The richest forests lay in the lower lands, readily accessible to loggers, and they were the first to be cut. The loggers were thorough and persistent in appropriating these forests. In Oregon only a few low-elevation watersheds remain uncut:

Oregon miner and activist George Atiyeh passes among trees with huge girths, some of which have been standing for hundreds of years. The path leads to Opal Creek, which became a rallying point for Atiyeh's family when the Forest Service announced plans to cut the area's trees.

Opal Creek, one of the best, still has eight-hundred-year-old trees that tower two hundred feet in the air. The Opal Creek stand is only three miles wide and eight miles long, a final bastion of Oregon's finest trees. And the Forest Service has sought to cut these, too.

National public lands in the Pacific Northwest are managed by either the U.S. Forest Service or the Bureau of Land Management, which arrange sales of timber from the lands they administer. Professional foresters officially establish the amount of timber to be sold and cut in any given year, but often Congress, at the behest of the lumber industry, tells forest managers how much timber to cut. The decisions are often based not on biological data but on political interests.

How much old growth remains in the Northwest is hotly disputed. Loggers say there is plenty. Rob Freres, president of Freres Timber Company in Lyons, Oregon, says: "We have seven million to twelve million acres of old growth in Oregon and Washington. We're not going to run out now or in the future, and the question is whether we use our land, whether we manage our lands, or we don't."

Jerry Franklin, a Forest Service botanist and a professor at the University of Washington, has a different view. The ancient forests are being rapidly depleted, he says. "You know, you hear all the time about the rate of deforestation of the tropical forest, and it's tremendous, and it's a catastrophe, but we have a much higher rate of forest cutting going on here in the Pacific Northwest."

Indeed, satellite data collected by the National Aeronautics and Space Administration indicate that the forests of Oregon and Washington are in worse shape than those of the Amazon. While the Amazon rain forest has been cut along its edges, much of the interior remains intact. The Pacific Northwest forests have been fragmented by innumerable small cuts that make it look like a moth-eaten blanket from the air. Much of the forest that remains is chopped into pieces too small to be of use to wildlife that depends on old growth, compounding the importance of saving the few remaining larger stands.

Although Washington State has three million acres set aside as protected wilderness areas, little of that, Franklin says, is ancient forest. He adds, "There's almost no significant old-growth forest preserved in the state of Oregon." Forest Service administrators disagree, alleging that some four million acres of ancient forest remain. The Forest Service, however, traditionally labels any stand of trees more than eighty years old as old growth. When forced to narrow the definition to prime virgin forest only, even the Forest Service admits that only 300,000 acres of the state's four million acres of remaining forest are protected ancient forest.

Ironically, and perhaps tragically, most of the logging done in national forests actually loses money for the federal government. The Forest Service claims that it brings in about $650 million yearly, but a 1991 special congressional assessment of Forest Service income showed a loss of nearly $200 million once costs including road building, boundary surveys, and funds paid out to counties were deducted. Road building is a major drain because under the terms of federal timber sales, it is the Forest Service's responsibility to build roads into the national forests to make the trees more accessible to loggers. The cost is immense, about $300 million yearly. But then, the service is one of the biggest road building organizations in the world—its road system is eight times the size of America's interstate highway system, and the service adds an average of forty-five hundred miles each year. When all costs are deducted, we discover that barely more than a dozen of the nation's roughly 160 national forests earn a profit from logging.

Why cutting continues at a loss in the nation's oldest forests during a time of critical federal budget deficits is abundantly clear. The logging industry, one of the larger employers in the Pacific Northwest, has dominated the region's economy for decades, making it a potent political force to which senators and representatives must pay attention. In addition, logging has other ardent supporters. One is the Forest Service itself—fifteen thousand of its thirty-five thousand employees are foresters, and although even they are beginning to see the value of protecting ancient forests, traditionally they have been trained to see trees as living lumber and ancient trees as a waste of land that could be used for faster-growing young trees. Moreover, their work depends on logging, predisposing them to support the timber industry. Other logging allies are the county governments in ancient-forest country—they receive a cut of the money generated by timber sales.

This coalition of economic and political interests once made it nearly impossible for conservationists to achieve stronger protection of the little remaining ancient forest. But in recent years the public has become more concerned about the nation's ecological integrity, and a large number of people have become increasingly vocal in their support of forest protection. As a result, the logging of the Pacific Northwest has evolved from a local into a national issue. This has made it much harder for local elected officials to force recklessly large cuts through Congress and the Forest Service.

In fact, local support of forest protection has nearly brought logging in the Pacific Northwest to a halt. This development began in 1988, when an Oregon chapter of the National Audubon Society requested that the northern spotted owl be added to the federal endangered species list. The timber industry was loath to see this happen, because clearly if the owl were listed, the Forest Service and the Bureau of Land Management could no longer plan cuts virtually heedless of their impact on wildlife. The industry tried to stop the listing, working through allies in the Reagan and Bush administrations. As a result, the U.S. Fish and Wildlife Service, the agency responsible for determining whether the owl should be listed, responded to political pressure and delayed its decision until ordered to make one by a federal court; only then was the owl listed as threatened.

Since the listing, the battle over the forests has centered around the owl. The owl, however, is not the issue: the forests are. The owl came to the fore only because the United States lacks any law for the express protection of endangered or vanishing ecosystems, in this instance the ancient forests of the Pacific Northwest. The nation does, however, have the Endangered Species Act, which makes it illegal for the federal government to fund or engage in activities that damage the habitat of a listed species. Because the owl is listed and biologists believe that logging of the ancient forests will reduce its numbers, any continued cutting of the

Logs are floated toward
an Oregon sawmill.
The once-proud trees
will then be stripped of
bark, and many will be
shaved into layers for
plywood. The cores will
be used for fenceposts.

forests will violate the Endangered Species Act. It is for this
reason that conservationists have turned to the owl as a
means of protecting the ancient forests.

But even after the owl was listed, the Bush administration
sought to evade federal laws requiring protection of the
forests. Lawsuits brought to federal court by the Seattle
Audubon Society charged the Forest Service and the Bureau
of Land Management with mismanagement of public lands,
eventually leading to a 1991 court decision that blocked 80
percent of Forest Service timber sales. In another decision,
bureau sales also nearly ground to a halt. In both cases, the
ruling district judge said the agencies had violated national
wildlife laws and failed to meet the standards of the
Endangered Species Act.

The unfortunate truth is that all the effort the Reagan
and Bush administrations put into the maintenance of logging led toward ultimate economic hardship for the average
working logger. The cuts of the 1980s were unsustainable,
gutting the ancient forests and robbing them from future
generations. If the Forest Service and the Bureau of Land
Management were to resume cutting as practiced in the
1980s, almost all the remaining virgin forest would be cut
within the next few years. This would put many loggers permanently out of work as well as undercut the tourist industry
that presently brings $6 billion yearly to Oregon and
Washington. The big timber companies, meanwhile, will sur-

Although the spotted owl has become a focal point in the debate over logging in national forests and other public lands, it is just one of thousands of species that have evolved in an old-growth environment. If that environment changes, the survival of these species can no longer be assured. (facing page)

vive. After the cheap federal timber has been cut, they can leave the area and cut forests overseas, as some are already doing in Southeast Asia, or log the second-growth forests that are maturing on the logging companies' own lands. Ironically, it is the aggressive practices of the 1980s that pose the greatest threat to logging jobs.

But then, timber companies have generally shown little concern for the way their business policies affect the local job market. Though the companies maintain that logging restrictions required by environmental concerns are causing unemployment, the main reason lies within the industry itself. Jobs in the Oregon-Washington wood products industry dropped from 133,400 in 1979 to scarcely 100,000 in 1986, even though timber production increased from 11.2 billion board feet to 12.3 billion. The reason: Automation of timber mills in the early eighties reduced the number of employees needed to produce a million board feet of lumber by roughly 35 percent.

Conservationists have long contended that economic problems in the Pacific Northwest can be solved not by more logging but by more processing of logs. The bulk of the trees felled in Oregon and Washington are shipped to Japan as raw logs or pulp. If logs were milled into lumber in Oregon and Washington, and even made into final products such as furniture, more jobs could be created with less forest destruction. In this regard, the United States could learn a lesson from Costa Rica, a Central American nation that is attempting to make economic use of its tropical rain forest while at the same time preserving it as a wildlife habitat. At least one Costa Rican company is also experimenting with procedures such as selective logging—in which only a few individually picked trees are cut in any area—rather than clear-cutting, in which everything is cut.

The economy of the Pacific Northwest may soon be moving in this direction. In early July 1993, President Clinton announced a new timber plan that would reduce logging to about one-fifth of the average rate from 1980 to 1992. The administration also plans to offer $1.2 billion in aid over a five-year period for work training and community assistance

and to remove federal subsidies that encourage the export of raw logs. The plan would establish reserves around rivers, streams, and areas critical to wildlife, though some thinning and salvage logging would be permitted in the reserves. The plan also calls for the establishment of ten study areas for experiments in marrying forest protection to economic use.

It is too early to know where this will lead. Initial reaction to the plan was mixed at best. Mark Rey, the American Forest and Paper Association's vice president for forest resources, said, "The Clinton administration has spent ninety days developing a solution to the crisis that will leave us exactly where we were when it began: court-ordered gridlock, with no timber being sold for the foreseeable future." Brock Evans, who works on timber issues for the National Audubon Society, took a contrary position: "This is the best deal the timber industry could get without breaking the law."

Evans's view was echoed by Carl Pope, executive director of the Sierra Club, who said: "With this proposal, the fate of the forests will stay in the hands of the very agencies that pushed them to the point of collapse. It is a sincere attempt to protect the remaining ancient forests, but the way it is crafted won't accomplish this goal." Karin Sheldon, president of the Wilderness Society, offered a more moderate interpretation while still expressing concern over the direction Clinton was taking. She said: "This is a great step forward, but we think the plan has some very serious flaws. . . . They are talking about reserves, but they are not inviolate. There will be pressure on the Forest Service to use salvage and thinning as a cover for harvest."

The fight over Pacific Northwest timber will go on. Congressional members from the area already have reported that they will seek legislation requiring higher timber cuts than Clinton proposes. The *Washington Post* reported that House Speaker Thomas Foley, a Washington State Democrat, has suggested that, "legislation might be needed that is not 'limited' by the administration goal of complying with existing environmental law." In other words, Foley may try to get national forests in the Pacific Northwest exempted from laws designed to protect them.

Clearly, logging of ancient forests will remain one of the

most polarizing of all environmental issues—as well it should, for the fate of those forests lies in the decisions our society is now making. As independent forestry consultant Chris Maser explains: "I see hope because we have the chance, in my opinion probably the last chance, here in the Northwest and in southwestern Canada, to learn how to sustain a temperate forest. We've got very fertile soils and very gentle climate and clean air. But if we lose it here, in my opinion, humanity loses it, because there's no place else that I know of where we can still do that."

Chapter Five

FRESH WATERS

ivers and lakes have long been centers of human activity and development. Rivers were vital to early agricultural peoples and in some places were worshipped, for in their ability to nurture crops, livestock, and people, they appeared to have the power of gods. In an age when travel was accomplished primarily on foot or with the aid of horses, rivers became highways along which boats could move with relative speed. Lakes provided people with permanent water supplies as well as a food source in the form of fish and shellfish.

So it is no surprise that when the first European colonists came to the New World, they settled along fresh waters, particularly rivers. Jamestown, Virginia, Britain's first permanent settlement, lay on the James River. New Amsterdam, the Dutch settlement that would become New York City, was born where the Hudson River meets the sea. Fort Duchesne, the French settlement that would become Pittsburgh, arose where two mountain rivers—the Allegheny and the Monongahela—converged to form the Ohio River.

The Ohio took on inestimable importance late in the eighteenth century and into the early nineteenth, when it became the main avenue by which settlers moved into the Northwest Territories, lands today encompassed by Minnesota, Michigan, Wisconsin, Illinois, and Indiana. Settlement of this area was critical after the American Revolution because it was the only way the new nation could hope to solidify its claim to the territories and ward off British intrusion.

The hopes of the nascent United States and its pioneers were tied to rivers. On rivers they sought the Northwest Passage, the fabled direct route to China; they built towns, farms, and ranches, laid out trade routes, and trapped furs for sale to Europe.

Since that time, most American rivers have aged badly.

Sunset on the Platte River near Grand Island, Nebraska, casts a quiet spell. Reduced flow from dams and diversions has changed the river's character and habitats. This has affected populations of whooping and sandhill cranes that stop over during migration. (facing page)

Large stretches have become deadly with toxins. A section of the Mississippi River near Baton Rouge has become known as Cancer Alley because human residents in the area suffer some of the nation's highest cancer rates. Many lakes, turned into repositories for human waste or sources of water for irrigation and household needs, have lost their original level of biological productivity. The Great Lakes in particular suffered as the cities along their shores dumped millions of gallons of waste into the water daily.

Pollution is not the only plague that agricultural and industrial use has brought to American waters. All of the nation's big rivers and most of its smaller ones are fettered with dams—primarily for agricultural purposes. As a result, the majority of our rivers no longer flow naturally, and some are so heavily taxed that they scarcely flow at all.

The problems that American fresh waters face are typical of those that beset rivers and lakes throughout the world. France is considering a plan to dam the Loire, which, though it has been diked along parts of its course, is considered Europe's last wild river. Europe's Rhine and Danube and India's Ganges have long histories of serious pollution. The problems we see in U.S. lakes and streams are merely the tip of a global iceberg.

Rivers and lakes take on the qualities of the lands that surround them because they are inextricably linked to those lands by rainfall. When rain or snow melt rushes across the Earth, it washes materials from the soil, carrying along particles of silt, chemicals, salts, and minerals. This runoff water may sink into the earth, dripping into vast underground reservoirs called aquifers, where pollution can linger for centuries. Or it may flow into lakes, rivers, and streams, which will carry pollution far and wide.

In cities, runoff carries industrial chemicals and other effluents and wastes, including chemicals used on suburban lawns. In farmlands, it is heavily laden with soil, pesticides, and fertilizers—the U.S. agricultural industry uses nearly 350 billion pounds of fertilizers yearly and 430 billion pounds of pesticides—as well as naturally occurring salts that build up to toxic levels in irrigation runoff. As a result, rivers, lakes, and the bodies of water they feed into become repositories of pollution.

For example, a U.S. Geological Survey done in the late 1980s found pesticides in 90 percent of tested streams in ten Midwestern states. A 1988 Environmental Protection Agency study detected forty-six farm pesticides in the wells of twenty-six states, and a 1986 report listed forty-seven states in which agricultural runoff was the main culprit in the loss of waterways for swimming and fishing. Nearly a quarter of drinking-water wells tested in Kansas and South Dakota exceeded federal health standards for nitrates, which are contaminants from fertilizers and pose serious health risks. In the late 1980s, the Iowa Department of Natural Resources sampled streams that previously had been treated to remove pesticide contamination. Results disclosed that pesticides remained in 60 percent of the samples. And at Kesterson National Wildlife Refuge in California, irrigation runoff channeled into the refuge to provide ponds for water-fowl was so contaminated with selenium, a toxic salt, that by the early 1980s, refuge personnel were chasing the birds away from the refuge for the animals' safety.

Probably no body of fresh water better illustrates the threats that contamination poses to the nation than do the Great Lakes. In 1615, French explorer Samuel de Champlain boated into Lake Huron and became the first European of record to see one of the Great Lakes. Misled by its size, he called it the Sweet Sea. Within the next fifty years, other Europeans traveled the region, tallying five bodies of water they recognized as lakes.

At that early date, settlers along the lakes were exclusively Native Americans who had little or no impact on the area's ecological integrity. But once the first Europeans arrived, that integrity began to break up. First on the scene were fur trappers, who succeeded in reducing populations of beavers, river otters, and other local furbearers. Later, the fledgling U.S. government granted some of its Great Lakes holdings to citizens whose property had been burned during the Revolutionary War.

Within fifty or sixty years after the Revolution, cities sprang up along the lakeshores, among them Cleveland,

Milwaukee, and Chicago. These and others were built along the short, sluggish rivers that fed into the lakes. Although these rivers did a poor job of moving along and dissipating wastes, the cities nevertheless dumped into them. Within a quarter century, waterways that early settlers had described as clear were reported to be turbid, even filthy. The problem was compounded when cities dredged canals and harbors, adding sediment to the rivers and lakes, and when loggers late in the nineteenth century deforested most lakeshores, causing erosion. Sawmills also dumped tons of sawdust into streams and lakes. As it decomposed, the sawdust used up oxygen in the lake water and killed off fish. The early twentieth century saw the arrival of industrial plants for the production of steel, aluminum, pesticides, and other goods, and the dumping of some three hundred toxins into surrounding waters. The steel industry dumped so much asbestos that the floor of Lake Superior's entire west arm is now carpeted with it.

Lake Erie shows the results of this abuse. By 1950, every major river draining into the lake was heavily polluted. For decades, Detroit and Buffalo had been dumping untreated sewage into it. The Detroit River poured in twenty million pounds of pollutants daily, ranging from nutrients such as phosphate and nitrogen to toxins such as phenols and chlorides. The Buffalo River was worse, so steeped in toxins that sludge worms, known for their resistance to poison, could not live in it. Its waters were clouded with coliform bacteria from human feces. By the late 1950s, biologists discovered that one 2,600-square-mile portion of Lake Erie had no dissolved oxygen in its bottom waters.

For years, politically powerful industrial and agricultural interests had held off serious change, but in the 1960s, the tide started to turn against them as the public demanded cleanup. Perhaps the breaking point for the public came in 1969, when the Cleveland stretch of the Cuyahoga River, which was iridescent with oil and other pollutants, burst into flames.

Support for public concern came from the International Joint Commission, which in 1970 published a report on pollution in lakes Erie and Ontario. The commission was created in 1909 to negotiate border disputes between the United States and Canada and continues to play a role in protecting

Pleasure boats ply the waters of Lake Erie. In the 1950s, when all major rivers draining into it were heavily polluted, Lake Erie was declared dead. Public outcry brought results, but today lake sediments are still packed with dangerous toxins. (facing page)

the lakes. Its 1970 report brought results in 1972, when the United States and Canada signed the International Great Lakes Water Quality Agreement, designed to help control phosphate flow into the Great Lakes. At the same time, cities, states, and provinces around the lakes concluded agreements for cleanup. In 1972, Congress enacted the Clean Water Act, which set standards for water quality and offered federal funding for improved wastewater treatment, and Canada set limits on phosphate effluents with passage of its Water Act.

This resulted in a noticeable improvement of the lakes by the mid-1970s. Waters were clearing up; phosphate flows

Flotsam and jetsam still turn up on Lake Erie beaches. While sewage dumping and the resultant algal blooms are events of the past in the Great Lakes, studies show that beneath the water's surface, all is not well.

into Lake Erie—the hardest hit of the five lakes—had been halved; algal blooms disappeared; and Lake Erie changed from green to blue. Fish once again swam in the previously moribund Detroit River, and the Cuyahoga ceased to be a fire hazard.

But despite improvements during the past two decades, serious pollution problems persist in the Great Lakes. Scientists from federal agencies such as the U.S. Fish and Wildlife Service and from a variety of universities have found that pollutants such as DDT and PCBs (polychlorinated biphenyls) remain at dangerously high levels, affecting many Great Lakes fish species, particularly the lake trout, a top predator. As a result of eating the fish, many bird species, such as cormorants and gulls, show high percentages of birth defects. The beluga whales of the St. Lawrence River, which receives flow from the Great Lakes as well as from point-source pollutants along its own shores, are so heavily contaminated that their reproductive rate is dropping and their population threatens to collapse. Some lake fish species fail to reproduce, and otters, bald eagles, and other fish-eaters along lakeshores are declining.

Human populations also are in jeopardy. Some data suggest that women who regularly eat Great Lakes fish are more susceptible to miscarriages than are women who avoid the fish. A study in the late 1980s by psychologists at Wayne State University indicates that the children of women who eat lake fish are smaller and less responsive during alertness tests than those of woman who do not eat the fish, apparently a result of fetal exposure to PCBs from the mother's blood during pregnancy.

The presence of toxins in the tissues of living fish suggests that many dangerous pollutants persist in the lakes despite cleanup efforts. These pollutants have filtered from the water into lake sediments, which makes their removal difficult if not impossible. The most obvious means for cleanup is dredging, but this stirs up sediment and actually risks putting pollutants back by water and increasing the likelihood of their absorption by flora and fauna.

The food chain remains laden with toxins. Wisconsin biologists found that 25 percent of the fish taken from the lakes is unsafe for consumption. Trout from Lake Superior, the least polluted of the lakes, bear 4 parts per million of PCBs in their tissues, twice the maximum the federal government considers safe for human consumption. In Lake Michigan, lake trout contain 36 parts per million of PCBs, eighteen times the maximum level that is safe for consumption. A study by the National Wildlife Federation in the late 1980s concluded that eating a single eight-ounce, skin-on fillet from a lake trout longer than thirty inches can raise a diner's risk of cancer tenfold, to 1 in 100,000. If a person eats one such meal a week, the risk rises to 1 in 10. It is unlikely that toxins in Great Lakes fish will be reduced in the near future. Consequently, the federal Food and Drug Administration has recommended that no one eat more than five pounds of Great Lakes fish yearly. The National Wildlife Federation, in its independent study, suggested that even this amount is too much by half.

While the level of toxins in fish serves as a stark warning of the dangers we face as a result of our pollution, another warning comes from Isle Royale, an island in Lake Superior. On Isle Royale lies Siskiwit Lake. Although the island, home to a national park, has never been farmed or developed—it is in fact a nearly pristine wilderness isolated from the world by the waters of Lake Superior—the sediments of Siskiwit Lake are laced with toxins, including dioxins, PCBs, and DDE, a by-product of DDT. Even more remarkable, scientists found in the mid-1980s that fish from Siskiwit bore twice the PCBs and ten times the DDE of fish from Lake Superior.

This isolated lake fell victim to contamination because it could not escape the wind. Studies of Siskiwit Lake's sediments indicate that pesticides first arrived there after World War II, when their use was first becoming widespread. By studying wind patterns, scientists also determined that Siskiwit's toxaphene—a pesticide used on crops—came from farms near Greenville, Mississippi, a source more than one thousand miles away. Scientists suspect that 80 percent of the PCBs in the Great Lakes arrived on the wind, along with an estimated yearly delivery of fifteen tons of PAHs (polycyclic aromatic hydrocarbons, byproducts of fossil-fuel burning).

To reverse damage done to the Great Lakes, the

International Joint Commission has urged the United States and Canada to stop the inflow of persistent pollutants and to make lake cleanup a priority, including restoration of polluted areas and increased public education. The public, meanwhile, is taking the situation into its own hands as citizens' groups apply themselves to the tasks of cleaning up the lakes and their tributary rivers. The Friends of the Buffalo River, for example, is helping to develop the type of comprehensive restoration plan called for by the Joint Commission.

One major source of water pollutants is gradually being limited by individual action. Some farmers have discovered that lowering the heavy use of pesticides and fertilizers can reduce costs and even boost production. In Arkansas, Agricultural Extension Service weed specialist Ford Baldwin reported in the late 1980s that chemical companies exaggerate the amount of fertilizers and herbicides that farmers need to use on their fields. "We found that we can cut herbicide rates down to about one fourth of those on the label [of an herbicide container]," Baldwin asserted, "if they're applied properly under the conditions we specify, and get results equivalent to a full rate, with no difference in yield at the end of the year." Glynn Brown, an Arkansas farmer, decided to try Baldwin's approach. In the first year, he halved his herbicide use and saved $8,000. "It was costing me about sixteen dollars an acre for one application of a particular chemical," he said. "With a reduced rate we went down to eight dollars an acre, and with these new chemicals now coming out we're going down even below that." He observed, though, that proper timing of the chemical applications is critical to success. "If you don't hit the right time and the right weather conditions, you're going to have to go back to that full rate." In 1986, more than one thousand Arkansas farmers tried Baldwin's technique and saved more than $2 million, creating benefits both for themselves and for the environment.

Pennsylvania farmer Paul Clugston took advantage of another program designed to reduce the use of chemical fertilizers by replacing them with an old standby, manure. Pennsylvania State University research on fertilizing with livestock manure supplemented with chemical fertilizer has taught Clugston to store manure produced by his livestock and spread it on his fields. This reduces the amount of both manure and chemical fertilizer that drains from fields into nearby streams. Clugston said, "Since we used our manure storage, which is in now for six years, we cut our fertilizer bill down by 65 percent. The economics part of it is a real factor to us, because of the slim margin of profit. Any penny we can save is a penny earned."

Combating many environmental problems, pollution among them, is often simply a matter of leaving old traditions behind and acting on new data. When many of the nation's leading industries started up, environmental laws were weak and ecological understanding was rudimentary. Since that time, science has shown us the costs and risks of continuing traditional industrial practices such as dumping effluents into rivers. However, businesses are often reluctant to adopt the new approaches and take the new precautions our increasing knowledge demands.

Much of this reluctance springs from the newness of our understanding of the damages human endeavors can bring to the health and safety of our environment. We live in a time of change, a time in which society is just beginning to recognize that many traditional approaches to doing business can no longer be sustained. This requires social, political, and economic adaptations, and puts some segments of society at odds with one another. This is particularly clear in the matter of dam projects, which historically have provided flood control and water for drinking and irrigation. Today, however, when most of the nation's rivers are dammed, the building of more dams and water projects has taken on a momentum of its own that often has little to do with need.

Somewhere between 64,000 and 80,000 dams have been constructed across the nation's 3.2 million miles of rivers. Designed to provide water for agricultural irrigation and urban use as well as power for generating electricity, the dams yield some negative results as well. In the Pacific Northwest, dams are a significant factor in the decline of salmon species that, once the foundation of a multimillion-dollar fishing industry and a subsistence base for local Native Americans, are now candidates for listing under the

Endangered Species Act. In 1991, the National Marine Fisheries Service placed the Snake River sockeye salmon on the endangered list because the fish had not been seen in its spawning waters for two years. Eight dams on the Columbia River, along which young salmon migrate from spawning beds in central Idaho to the sea, kill 93 percent of the fish, which are ground up in turbines or stopped by the dams.

In other areas, the rivers themselves are disappearing. Irrigation projects draw so much water each year from the Colorado River, which during countless eons has carved the Grand Canyon into northern Arizona, that now the river is scarcely a trickle where it runs into the Gulf of California, and the life once supported in its lower reaches is gone. The area that was probably the Colorado's greatest stretch of rapids lies drowned today beneath the placid waters of Lake Mead. Similarly, the Great Falls of the Missouri River, whose eighteen miles of rapids and cataracts awed Meriwether Lewis as the Lewis and Clark expedition moved across Montana in 1804, also lie lost beneath a reservoir.

Many of the dams were built for what seemed to be perfectly good reasons, such as turning dry lands into croplands or using the force of flowing water to provide electricity for cities. The Colorado, for instance, provides half the drinking water of Los Angeles and Phoenix. But in many cases the rivers have been harnessed too severely. Nebraska's Platte River is one such example.

The Platte River tumbles out of the Rockies clear, cold, and foaming. It travels in two branches, the North Platte flowing north out of Colorado into Wyoming before turning east into Nebraska, and the South Platte emerging from the Rockies to roll across the eastern Colorado plains before meeting the North Platte in western Nebraska to form the Platte, which runs east through Nebraska to the Missouri River.

Six diversion dams encumber the South Platte today. Another six lie on the main stem of the North Platte. Every year, nearly 1.5 million acre-feet of water (an acre-foot of water is enough to cover an acre with a foot of water, or to meet the water needs of the average U.S. family for two years) drawn from the North Platte Valley are used to irrigate some 325,000 acres of land.

The most significant dangers to wildlife came with the completion of two dams in 1941. The Kingsley Dam on the North Platte, just west of the river's meeting with the South Platte, retains a 1.7-million-acre-foot reservoir, Lake McConaughy. Branching out from Lake McConaughy are some five hundred miles of canals that transport water to Nebraska farms as far as two hundred miles away.

The Tri-County Diversion Dam sits just below the meeting point of the North and South Plattes. Though it is the only dam on the main stem of the Platte, it controls the entire flow of water into eastern Nebraksa.

Before the dams were built, the rush of sediment-laden water scoured the riverbed during high water, keeping banks free of trees and keeping islands and sandbars clear of vegetation. Today, Lake McConaughy captures fully 70 percent of the river's flow and its sediment. As a result, the river channel, which once ranged up to three miles wide, has shrunk. Sections that spanned 2,200 yards in 1866 now average less than 100 yards. Trees are closing in on the river's banks, and sandbars and islands are becoming overgrown with cottonwoods and willows. Analyses of annual tree rings suggest that the trees' biggest advances began with the closing of the gates of Kingsley Dam.

The shrinking of the river and the influx of trees is ruining the Platte for native wildlife, particularly the flocks of lesser sandhill cranes that come every spring to the stretch of the Platte called Big Bend, which lies in south-central Nebraska. The sandhill cranes stand about three feet tall, have six-foot wingspans, and fly to the Platte in March like an invading air force, about half a million of them filling the skies with their gray silhouettes and chattering calls. This is the world's largest single gathering of cranes. Before it is over—the entire sojourn runs roughly six weeks—about 80 percent of the continent's total sandhill crane population will have rested along the Platte during the long spring migration that takes the birds from Texas, New Mexico, Mexico, and parts of the Gulf Coast all the way to the Arctic.

While on the Platte, the cranes feed and fatten, spending more than half their daylight hours in the croplands that border the river, eating corn left after the previous harvest—

Lesser sandhill cranes are among the wildlife that relies on the wide, shallow Platte River for food and protection during migratory stopovers. Proposed water projects would further reduce the river's flow, eliminating vital roosting areas.

about fifteen hundred tons in all, providing the birds with about 90 percent of their weight gain while on the Platte. Farmers welcome them, since they eat only loose kernels lying on the ground, which are of no interest to cattle. The cranes also feed in hayfields and native grasslands, getting protein and minerals from earthworms, snails, and other invertebrates.

This stopover is essential to the cranes' survival. They will burn off nearly half their accumulated energy during the subsequent weeks of flying that bring them to their Arctic nesting ground. What is left sustains them while nesting.

The cranes come to Big Bend because it gives them the type of roost they require—open, unvegetated river channels a thousand feet wide—and convenient feeding areas. Here they can spot predators and other dangers, and the water is deep enough to shelter them from raccoons, coyotes, dogs, and other enemies.

Thousands of people come to the Platte each year, drawn by the cranes. One favored roost for birders is the National Audubon Society's two-thousand-acre Lillian Annette Rowe Sanctuary, where guided field trips and blinds provide close-up looks at the cranes as they come and go from their roosting areas in the Platte, floating down on outstretched wings. One birder said of the experience: "It's like one of the ten wonders of the world. There's no place else in the world that we have the privilege to see this."

But this experience may soon be lost, for the crane's wetland habitat is threatened on all sides, from North Dakota to west Texas, as irrigation drains it away. Colorado, Nebraska, and Wyoming all have plans for diverting even more of the Platte's water, further jeopardizing the crane's habitat.

In recent years, the greatest threat has been a water project called Two Forks Dam, which the City of Denver wanted to construct on the South Platte River in the Rocky Mountains. Although the dam was first proposed in the 1930s, nothing actually happened until the 1970s, when oil fields near Denver attracted a burgeoning number of new residents. City officials feared that rapid growth would yield a water shortage, so they began to push the federal government for permits to build Two Forks. Then, in 1985, oil development dropped off, Denver's growth stopped, and fears of water shortages seemed increasingly unrealistic. Yet pressure to build the dam mounted.

This was because of a law, enacted in 1974 by the Colorado State Legislature, that made it virtually impossible for Denver to annex more land, thus cutting off growth of the city's tax base. As the city found it increasingly difficult to meet its budget, it considered the option of selling water to nearby towns by building the Two Forks reservoir. According to U.S. Army Corps of Engineers figures, if the dam had been built, 65 percent of its water would have been used by single-family homes, with more than half of that amount being used for watering lawns.

In exchange for the greener lawns, Colorado would have lost a state-designated Gold Medal trout stream, nearly ten thousand acres of deer habitat, six hundred of elk habitat, and up to a third of the entire population of the threatened Pawnee montane skipper butterfly, whose habitat would be drowned. According to the U.S. Fish and Wildlife Service, the last remaining bighorn sheep population within the Two Forks project area probably would be eliminated as well.

Those were the expected effects within the area surrounding the dam. But the dam's influence would reach far beyond the Rockies, across five hundred miles to the Platte River's Big Bend, where it was thought likely that the water impoundment would reduce flows below the critical threshold required by sandhill cranes and other wildlife. This would have been compounded by a Wyoming plan to build a dam on Deer Creek, a tributary of the North Platte. The U.S. Fish and Wildlife Service, which examined the project as required under the Endangered Species Act to measure its possible effects on listed species, said the impoundment would jeopardize whooping cranes and other listed birds unless the Deer Creek sponsors promised to use bulldozers and other heavy equipment to remove vegetation from twenty-four acres in the Platte and to widen its channel. To accomplish this objective, Wyoming also purchased 470 acres of crane habitat in Nebraska, which the U.S. Fish and Wildlife Service agreed to restore and maintain. However, a suit brought by the State of Nebraska, which itself coveted the water, led to a ruling that has temporarily blocked the dam on the grounds that the Endangered Species Act requires the federal government to protect a habitat, not trade it for artificially maintained areas.

The threat posed by Two Forks was removed in the late 1980s, when the Environmental Protection Agency, which issues the permits needed for dam construction, ruled that Two Forks could not be built. This was the result of a long battle fought by the National Audubon Society and other conservation groups not only in behalf of sandhill cranes and the thousands of people who enjoy the spectacle of their migration, but also because of the threats the dam posed to other wildlife and wildlife habitats, including some seven million to nine million ducks and geese that crowd the Platte during spring migration; millions of ducks that use the river in winter, when it sometimes provides the only open water in the area; about two hundred bald eagles that winter there, feeding on fish; the endangered whooping crane and endangered least tern; and a threatened population of piping plovers, all reduced by habitat loss.

While Two Forks has been canceled, the Platte and its

wildlife are still not safe. As soon as the Environmental
Protection Agency blocked Two Forks, the State of Nebraska
started pushing for its own plan, the Prairie Bend Project,
which would transfer 120,000 acre-feet of water from the
Platte River to southern Nebraska—twice as much as Deer
Creek would have claimed. The future for sandhill cranes,
whooping cranes, least terns, piping plovers, and other Platte
River wildlife thus remains inescapably linked to the designs
of water users who have already laid claim to 70 percent of
the river's flow.

The Prairie Bend Project is not the only new proposal for
redistributing the Platte. Fourteen projects proposed in
Colorado, Wyoming, and Nebraska call for putting 369,000
new acres of land under irrigation at a cost of at least $3 bil-
lion. The flow of water in the Platte would be reduced to
nearly zero.

Nationwide, dams sprout rapidly. In 1986, when even the
Reagan administration was trying to reduce federal dam
building, Congress authorized nearly three hundred new
water projects, including dams and drainages. Many are
unnecessary, such as a plan by the U.S. Army Corps of
Engineers to drain one hundred square miles of seasonal
Mississippi wetlands important to waterfowl in order to plant
crops such as cotton, soybeans, and wheat, all marginally
profitable and already grown in surplus.

Water conservation could remove the need for many
water projects. Indeed, the conservation of agricultural water
is the surest means for protecting the nation's water
resources, because irrigation accounts for roughly 80 percent
of all U.S. water use. According to the *Audubon Wildlife
Report 1987*, reducing western agricultural water use by 7 to
10 percent would eliminate the need for any new water
sources even if all other uses doubled. Conservation is also
critical for wildlife, because many of the nation's rivers are so
taxed by existing water projects that they will no longer
meet the basic needs of native species if required to meet
greater human demands for water.

Unfortunately, because present law requires those with
water rights to use their water or lose it, farmers who conserve irrigation water are penalized and wasting water is

encouraged. This is an economic tragedy as well as an ecological catastrophe because water conservation is a key means for reducing the costs of agricultural overhead. But hope for rivers has risen on the political horizon. Some 230 dams in fifty-nine river basins are presently awaiting renewal of federal operating permits. The federal government is likely to use this occasion for requiring dam administrators to better meet the needs of wildlife, including the construction of fish ladders or other means for moving salmon around dams. The salmon problem is likely to turn into a major political fight in the Pacific Northwest. This issue, like logging in the same area, involves complex ecological and economic issues that make compromise difficult.

As Ken Strom, manager of Audubon's Lillian Annette Rowe Sanctuary, points out about the Platte (and his words are true of many American rivers and their native wildlife): "We're at the point where we simply can't compromise anymore. The cranes can't compromise. The waterfowl can't compromise. They have no place else to go. And it's a very little concession for us to simply leave what's here in the river intact so that those who follow will still be able to enjoy the spectacle of the cranes."

Chapter Six

Coasts and Seas

The oceans that lap against our shores unite all the continents and islands of our planet into a single community, in which the actions of one nation can directly affect the health and well-being of another. Yet human society has long used the oceans as a dumping ground, as if by sinking our waste beneath the waves we could somehow lose it forever. Rather than disappearing, however, our wastes linger in the oceans and wash across the globe, posing an enduring threat to human health and to the marine environment. This can be seen in the heavily polluted North Sea, where sea lions have died in great numbers. It can be seen in the sewage that ocean waves carry from Mexican coasts to California shores. It can be seen in the global decline of coral reefs, a signal that ocean pollution has reached critical levels.

Debris—from glass bottles and plastic bags to lumps of oil—can be found on practically any U.S. beach. Every year, barges dump nine million tons of sewage sludge at the New York Bight disposal site, which lies only 106 miles offshore. Chemical companies pour millions of gallons of contaminated wastewater into the waters off the New Jersey Shore every day. Besides deliberate waste discharges, accidental releases occur—according to the U.S. National Research council, an average of 600,000 barrels of oil spilled yearly from tankers and other sources between 1975 and 1985. An additional twenty-one million barrels of petroleum products reach the ocean each year from street runoff, industrial effluents, the flushing of ships' tanks, and other sources.

The total amount of sewage and industrial waste, much of it tainted by chemical toxins, released into U.S. rivers and coastal waters each year stands at about 16 trillion gallons. Given this volume, it certainly is not surprising that New York City beaches are littered with garbage regurgitated by the ocean. But even areas far from human population centers

Cruise ships dock at a Caribbean port. Some of these floating hotels have been known to dump bag after bag of garbage at sea. (facing page)

A Staten Island beach is thick with debris. Home to Fresh Kills, the world's largest landfill, this borough of New York City is surrounded by major industry and shipping. As a result its beaches are unsafe for swimming and its seafood is considered unfit for human consumption. (facing page)

are showing signs of trouble. A three-year study of garbage reaching Sable Island, which lies about one hundred miles off Nova Scotia, shows how rapidly ocean currents can bring debris to distant shores. Each of the six beach sites selected for the study was about a third of a mile long and lay on the island's north side, where most debris washed in. During the study, which began in the late 1980s, volunteers removed all debris from the sites in April and collected new debris every forty days through November. During the three-year study, the volunteers picked up 11,183 items, an average of nearly 2,000 per mile. Ninety-four percent of the debris was plastic. Fishing gear made up about 35 percent of the total. Glass and metal products accounted for 5 and 1 percent, respectively.

Recently, scientists in the National Oceanic and Atmospheric Administration, a federal agency in the Department of Commerce, examined two hundred U.S. marine sites and concluded—to no one's surprise—that the worst pollution occurs in areas with large populations and heavy industrial development. Areas suffering the effects of coastal pollution include New York and Boston harbors, Chesapeake Bay, Puget Sound, San Franciso Bay, San Diego Harbor, and much of the Gulf of Mexico.

Pollution has had far-reaching effects on thousands of lives. Alaska loses as many as thirty thousand northern fur seals yearly to entanglement in fishnet debris; the fur seal population has dropped by half in the past thirty years and appears to be losing 4 to 8 percent of its numbers yearly. Commercial fishing is banned in Boston Harbor because the fish are too contaminated for human consumption. New York health officials have warned against eating bass, carp, sunfish, catfish, and walleye from the Hudson River, which empties into the ocean at New York Harbor. Striped bass from the Hudson River and New York Harbor, which in 1973 produced a catch of nearly 15 million pounds, are now so laden with toxins, including cancer-causing polychlorinated biphenyls (PCBs), that they are banned from commercial markets. Roughly 40 percent of shellfish beds across the United States have been closed to collection because of pollutants; in Washington State's Puget Sound, commercial catching of shellfish has been restricted in sixteen thousand

acres of shellfish beds. The Natural Resources Defense Council reported recently that 1992 saw twenty-six hundred beach closings because of public health threats from contamination. When we examine specific coastal sites, the magnitude and extent of the pollution that has led to these problems rapidly become apparent.

During recent presidential campaigns, Boston Harbor turned into a hotly debated political issue because of its severe and long-standing pollution. Each day, Boston dumps roughly 500 million gallons of treated sewage into its harbor, a volume that, according to the Massachusetts Water Resources Authority, equals the combined flow of the nearby Charles, Mystic, and Neponset rivers. Although the waste has been processed, about 10 percent of human wastes and 30 percent of toxins present in the raw sewage remain when the water is discharged.

This problem is compounded when untreated sewage gets into the harbor and into rivers around Boston. This happens in at least two ways. First, it leaks persistently from the five thousand miles of underground pipes—some of them more than one hundred years old and made of deteriorating wood—that carry sewage from more than forty surrounding communities to the Boston sewage treatment plants. Second, during heavy rains the system's drainage pipes over-flow, allowing raw sewage to flow directly into the harbor and its rivers. It is no wonder that Boston Harbor is off-limits to commercial fishermen, who now go more than seventy-five miles offshore to ensure a catch of uncontaminated fish.

Long Island Sound also suffers from coastal pollution run amok. The sound is a narrow body of marine water, covering some thirteen hundred square miles, that lies between the hundred-mile-long north shore of Long Island and the coasts of New York State and Connecticut. Every day the sound is hit with one billion gallons of waste water from forty New York and Connecticut sewage-treatment plants and an additional two million gallons of raw sewage. This is a daily average of roughly 800,000 gallons of sewage for every square mile of Long Island Sound.

Much of this waste is rich in plant nutrients, and once in

the sound they spur the reproduction of microscopic algae, which rapidly drain the water of dissolved oxygen. During the summer of 1987, dissolved oxygen in the western third of the sound fell so low that some 800,000 fish died, posing a financial threat to commercial fishermen. Three years later, dissolved oxygen in the five hundred square miles between the Bronx and New Haven dropped nearly to zero. Contamination by raw sewage has also led to fishing closures or restrictions on 146,000 acres of the sound's potential shellfish beds, representing a yearly loss in excess of $15 million for Connecticut alone.

Ten percent of all the people in the United States live within fifty miles of Long Island Sound, and land development has reached record levels. In the past three decades, nearly 70 percent of the upland areas along the sound's western half have been developed. Since colonial times, half the area's wetlands—which would have helped filter pollutants out of runoff—have been drained, much of it since the 1950s. The increase in development and housing, combined with the loss of the wetlands, has boosted the amount of urban runoff that reaches the sound. This is a clear danger, since urban runoff dumps far more contaminants, such as oil and gasoline washed from road surfaces, into rivers and seas than do all the tanker spills of any given year.

As Terry Backer, the official keeper of the sound and third-generation fisherman, explains, we rarely think about the tiny spills for which we are all responsible and which take a toll on the environment. "When you think about oil, you think about the Amoco Cadiz, you think about the Exxon Valdez, you think about the big, big oil spills," says Backer, referring to two American petroleum company tankers that made history with their massive oil spills. "But we have a continual oil spill on our coast. It happens every day. We have millions and millions of cars going up and down the road leaking hydrocarbon products—oil, grease, gasoline, ethylene-glycol antifreeze. All this stuff goes down to the road, and you know it doesn't disappear. And when it rains it comes down these storm drains and into the sound. We're the top of the food chain. We're the people who get it all in the end." The problem is compounded by increased industrial development, whose toxic chemical effluents have required states to close commercial shellfishing in particularly hazardous areas.

Ironically, another leading area of coastal pollution lies in Washington, a state to which many people are now retreating to escape the problems, such as pollution, that plague city life. Yet Puget Sound, which washes the shores of Seattle and Tacoma in Washington and Vancouver, and Victoria in British Columbia, stands out as one of the nation's most polluted bodies of water. The pollution has come from the usual sources—runoff, pollutants washed from the air during rain, and the industries and sewage treatment plants that annually dump some 100 million gallons of effluent into the sound. The sound encompasses two Superfund sites, which are toxic hot spots that the federal government has designated as the nation's worst pollution problems. In fact, Commencement Bay, near Tacoma, was the first underwater Superfund site.

Much of the evidence for this contamination comes from studies of Puget Sound wildlife. One fish species, the English sole, has been particularly useful to researchers because it is territorial, staying in one place and living on or under sediment. This makes it relatively easy to draw a correlation between the sole's physical condition and the condition of its environment. Toxicologists have found a high incidence of liver cancer in English sole from areas of highly contaminated sediments. Some evidence also suggests that toxins are contributing to reproductive failures in English sole and other flatfish.

Biochemist Donald Malins, who has studied the English sole, remembers: "When we discovered these problems about fifteen or more years ago, people said it wasn't so. People would say, 'You scientists, I mean you'd better go back and take a look at your notebooks, you're crazy. This is a pristine environment. With these tumors, I mean, what is it? It's nothing but alarmism. You're just an alarmist.' Well, it turned out that they reflected serious pollution problems in Puget Sound. We've got Superfund sites in Commencement Bay and in Eagle Harbor. It is not a fantasy of mine. It's not an issue of being an alarmist. It's a real problem."

During subsequent years, researchers have found potentially dangerous levels of PCBs and pesticides in killer whales along the Washington shore. These whales have experienced high incidences of premature births and deaths of pups in areas around the sound. During the same period, glaucous-winged gulls, pigeon guillemots, and great blue herons—three species that at several Puget Sound sites have suffered pesticide-induced egg-shell thinning and reproductive failure—have also shown some of the world's highest recorded levels of DDT contamination. If these are not warnings enough of human health threats, official actions have made the threat clear: In the past decade, contamination has forced the state to restrict the commercial harvest of shellfish in more than sixteen thousand acres of shellfish beds.

Toxins reach these animals in the foods they eat. The process begins with tiny creatures that feed on contaminated

A factory in Tacoma Bay, Washington, produces paper for grocery bags and other uses. Many paper-makers are notorious polluters, producing dioxin as a by-product of the bleaching process. Several Superfund sites have been linked to paper-makers, shipping industries, and wood-preserving plants in the Seattle-Tacoma area.

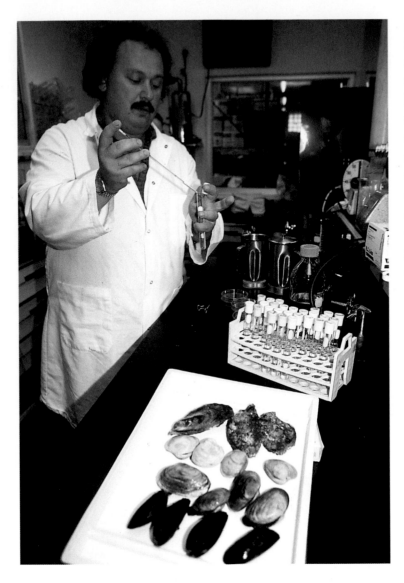

A scientist at Boston's Legal Seafoods tests shellfish for bacteria. Owner Roger Berkowitz buys seafood only from boats working at least eighty miles offshore. The restaurant boasts a stringent testing procedure for all its merchandise, which is quarantined for twenty-four hours after purchase.

sediments. They in turn are eaten by larger creatures, which are eaten by still larger creatures, until finally the toxins reach the end of the food chain. The greatest concentrations of these toxins per pound of body weight are in the animals at the end of the food chain, such as sea lions, bald eagles, seagulls, and humans. "In other words, it comes back to haunt you," says Malins. "It's coming back because human beings are part of the aquatic food chain. They eat fish. The toxins are not flushed from the body over time, but rather linger in fatty tissue and some organs. For this reason, even eating small quantities of toxified foods can ultimately be dangerous to one's health."

With the nation flanked by pollution problems in a very literal sense, the situation seems dire. Yet cause for optimism does exist. After all, when twenty-six hundred beaches are closed because of pollution, as they were in 1992, the public is going to take notice. And once the public begins to demand a solution to the problem, its outcry becomes a powerful tool for effecting change.

This has worked to an extent at Puget Sound. Better water treatment and recently imposed limits on industrial discharges have helped to reduce pollution. The yearly overflow of raw sewage has dropped from an average of 20 billion gallons in the 1950s to 2 billion gallons in the late 1980s. Officials predict an additional 75 percent decline by 1995. The sound's sediments are the worst remaining problem. PCBs, heavy metals, and other toxins that accumulate in sediments are a persistent danger because they can last for years or centuries, and if sediment is dredged, they can once again enter the water. However, industrial research into chemicals that will render the toxins harmless is under way in many private laboratories across the nation, offering some promise for the future removal of contaminants that now lie beyond our reach.

Puget Sound has been particularly fortunate because state and local officials as well as private citizens are committed to solving its problems. The state has set standards for identifying hazardous sediments and has developed a program for safely cleaning designated sites. Seattle uses a force of "sewer ranger patrols" to monitor underground sewer pipes, trace any toxins to their sources, and stop them before they enter the sound. Rather than dump treated sewage sludge into the sound, the city uses it as fertilizer. Local citizens have "adopted" streams, cleaning out debris and restoring damaged plant growth. One stream cleaner, Debbera Stecher, says: "We're cleaning our stream because we have to care. . . . Conservation starts here. It starts today. It starts in my own stream in my own park."

A combination of citizen and state endeavors has helped

reduce pollution in another problem area, Chesapeake Bay.
One of the nation's leading sources of shellfish, the bay is
also the recipient of river flows from Pennsylvania,
Maryland, and Virginia, flows that include massive amounts
of fertilizers and pesticides from farmlands. This has led to
contamination of commercial fish populations, such as the
striped bass, as well as declines in shellfish beds and other
commercially important species.

Fortunately the bay has been the beneficiary of help from
both citizens and bureaucrats. Both Maryland and Virginia
have enacted laws designed to reduce wetlands loss, helping
to ensure that runoff will filter through cleansing marshes
and swamps. New sewage-treatment facilities have reduced
pollutants in the Potomac River, which flows past
Washington, D.C., and between Maryland and Virginia.
Phosphorus effluents—the type of fertilizing compounds that
have depleted oxygen in parts of Long Island Sound—have
dropped from more than 8 million pounds yearly in the
1960s to 63,000 pounds in the late 1980s. Additional protections for the bay are the direct result of efforts by a citizen
action group called the Chesapeake Bay Foundation. Its
twenty-five years of work with regional politicians has led to
special restrictions on the taking of striped bass, helping to
stem a decline in bass numbers.

Boston Harbor also is benefiting from a municipal cleanup
effort: the construction of a massive new sewage treatment
plant, scheduled to open before the year 2000, which will
cost $6 billion and stand as the largest public work ever
undertaken in New England. It will reduce the amount of
sludge dumped into the harbor and will increase the amount
of sludge that can be processed into fertilizer. This will have
the added benefit of reducing the amount of sludge that is
presently trucked to New York landfills, which are likely to
overload within twenty-five years. Paul Levy, director of the
Massachusetts Water Quality Authority, says, "I'm cautiously
optimistic about the Boston situation. . . . Boston has awak-
ened. It's starting to fix its problems and make a lot of
investments."

So is Long Island Sound. In 1986, Terry Backer helped
create the Connecticut Coastal Fishermen's Association, an

activist alliance of fishermen, lobstermen, boat owners, and swimmers. That same year, the association sued the cities of Norwalk and Bridgeport when their sewage flows forced the closing of Norwalk's oyster beds. A year later, charged with 5,400 violations of the federal Clean Water Act, Norwalk settled out of court by agreeing to replace and repair its sewage-treatment equipment and pay a fine of $172,500. Half of that amount was earmarked for cleaning Norwalk Harbor and half for hiring a soundkeeper who would look for and report incidents of pollution and other problems. The idea for the soundkeeper came from the establishment in 1984 of a Hudson River keeper. Within the first two years, the Hudson's riverkeeper had won a $1.5-million suit against Exxon for polluting the river. The origin of the Hudson's riverkeeper can be traced to an old English custom of assigning special guards to monitor the condition of streams belonging to the Crown.

Terry Backer has since led legal battles resulting in multi-million-dollar improvements to area waste-treatment plants. He believes his commitment to the sound has as much to do with future generations as with the sound itself. "When my son Jacob was born," he says, "I looked around and saw that each generation was leaving less behind it, and I felt it was my responsibility to put up a fight for him. Maybe it has more to do with my kids than it has to do with the sound. The sound has certainly provided for me and my dad and my family for a long time. I mean we owe it, we owe it something."

Two people who seem to agree with Backer's commitment to clean costal waters are Bruce and Susan Bingham, who took individual action to stop illegal ocean dumping. Their effort began with a cruise off Florida's Atlantic coast. One evening as they watched the sea passing behind the ship, they were shocked to see the crew throwing plastic bags full of garbage overboard. "It was the perfect night," recalled Bruce. "Full moon and stars, and the ship was rolling gently, and the next thing we know, kersplash, kersplash! And there's a wake of garbage as far as we can see. It was actually coming out of both sides of the ship at once."

When the Binghams returned to their Florida home, they

helped start a campaign to reduce the dumping of plastic and other wastes into offshore waters and kicked off a media and letter-writing campaign that alerted Floridians to cruise ships' dumping. Eventually, in the face of bad press and public pressure, at least one cruise line agreed to stop dumping.

Another individual who is committed to the environment is actor Ted Danson, formerly of the television series *Cheers*. In the late 1980s, Danson visited a California beach near Los Angeles, and what he saw opened his eyes to the need for active environmental protection. "I've always considered myself an environmentalist, but in a passive sort of way," he says. "I began turning toward activism the day I took my daughters to Santa Monica Beach and discovered it was closed due to sewage pollution. I was outraged and frustrated. And I felt motivated to do something."

What he did was fund the creation of a new environmental group, the American Oceans Campaign, to work on marine problems. The organization, which has offices in Los Angeles and Washington, D.C., has become a leader in the fight to protect our marine shores. Danson himself has become increasingly informed about marine issues and has testified before Congress in behalf of ocean protection. "I have learned that our coasts are in peril and must be saved," he says. "I have seen the beginnings of a national change of attitude, a growing awareness that this problem is hurting all of us and that we all need to pitch in to solve it. I know that we need to pressure our leaders to make the environment a major national priority."

To do this, Danson observes, requires "a national will, a national desire to save the oceans. The only way that can happen is if individual people think that they can make a difference. If they don't think they can make a difference as individuals, then they will wait for somebody else to do it. Somebody else can't do it. It really has to be individuals who know that they can make a difference who will turn the tide."

Chapter Seven

Wetlands

In 1905, a Florida governor with the unlikely name of Napoleon Bonaparte Broward set out to accomplish a dream: He would drain the Florida Everglades, the largest freshwater marsh in the world, and turn it into farmland and development sites.

The idea, however, did not begin with Broward. It dated at least to 1850, when Congress passed the Swamp Lands Act, offering to give the states wetlands administered by the federal government provided that the states would fund drainage projects with money raised from the sale of the lands. However, before the earliest Everglades drainage plan could even be attempted, the Civil War intervened, and Florida was on the losing side. Not until 1882 did the first major drainage project get under way in southern Florida, and then it soon became clear that the technology of the era was simply not up to the task.

By the time Broward came on the scene, technology had greatly improved. He persuaded the state legislature to create a special Everglades Drainage Commission with broad powers for funding and carrying out drainage. He himself manned a dredge to raise the first shovelful of muck, beginning a long process to cut canals through the Everglades and run its water off into the ocean.

At first, Broward's perseverance and all-out assault on the Everglades—the Drainage Commission even approved the use of dynamite for blowing out river bottoms to improve the rivers as drainage channels—seemed to pay off. Land suitable for growing crops began to emerge from the marsh. When Broward left office at the end of the century's first decade, he had become known as "the man who drained the Everglades."

Around 1911, however, Everglades ecology reasserted itself, and Broward's achievement evaporated—or, rather,

The sun sets behind two wading birds near the mouth of the Mississippi River. Loss of wetlands in Louisiana, Florida, and many other states is one likely reason why duck and wading bird populations have declined in recent years. In Louisiana alone, 750,000 acres of marsh have disappeared in the past twenty-five years (facing page).

drowned. Heavy rains flooded much of the drained land, and it soon became clear that Broward had succeeded only because the Everglades had been experiencing an unrecognized dry spell.

Nevertheless, the Everglades was on its last legs. Soon it would succumb to twentieth-century engineering. In this regard it is symbolic of all wetlands destruction in the United States. When the first European settlers arrived in North America, the area covered by the lower forty-eight states encompassed about 230 million acres of wetlands. Today, about half of those wetlands have been drained or filled, and another three hundred thousand acres are continuing to disappear each year.

"Wetlands" is the generic word for swamps and marshes. Biologists and professional environmentalists have been saying for years that wetlands are vitally important to human society because they filter pollutants from rain runoff—the water that runs off the land after storms—and even from rivers and streams that flow through wetlands. Marshes, which are temporarily or permanently submerged grasslands, and swamps, which are temporarily or permanently submerged woodlands, slow the flow of water, allowing toxins to filter into the soil, from which they are then removed by plants. Thus, wetlands block the flow of toxins, both natural and human-caused, helping to cleanse our water supplies and croplands.

A river otter near Florida's Big Cypress National Park eats a sunfish. Many otters, beavers, and other mammals depend upon the wetlands for food and habitat.

In addition, wetlands serve as nurseries and habitat for many valuable species. Furbearers such as otters, beavers, muskrats, and mink are closely tied to or dependent upon wetlands. Even more importantly, many marine fish species use estuaries—where freshwater meets the sea—as nurseries for their young. This is true of wetlands around the Chesapeake Bay and along the Gulf of Mexico, of the mangrove stands of the Florida coast, and of the salt marshes of San Franciso Bay. Here a range of species—from sharks to the fish they feed upon, including many species of commercial value—start their lives.

Today, about 100 million acres of the lower forty-eight states' original wetlands remain. Of the many drainage and dam projects involved in wiping out more than half the original wetlands, none stands out so much as that which took place in the Everglades, now one of the nation's most disturbed ecosystems.

Perhaps the first thing a visitor notices about the Everglades on a clear spring day is the sky. It seems the widest sky in the world, stretching to eternity on all sides because the land is so flat and low, a green table of sawgrass punctuated with scattered stands of trees. Caught between this wide land and broad sky, the visitor feels the emptiness of the place.

Of course, the element that makes the Everglades what it is, is water. Water provides the sawgrass with the substrate and nutrients it needs; provides thousands of alligators and a few hundred crocodiles with the medium in which they live, feed, and breed; provides thousands of long-legged wading birds—egrets, wood storks, herons—with fish and a rugged habitat in which to nest. Without water, the Everglades would die, as we are learning after years of robbing the ecosystem of its precious fluid.

South Florida is a land of heavy rains, the May to September wet season bringing as much as sixty-three inches of downpour to some parts of the state. Under natural conditions, water reached the Everglades not only in rainfall but as overflow from a chain of lakes about two hundred miles north. During the rainy season, these lakes would flood the Kissimmee River Basin and send overflow into shallow Lake

Okeechobee, which lies in the central portion of the state and which, covering seven hundred square miles of surface area, ranks as the largest body of fresh water in the United States south of the Great Lakes. When Okeechobee was full, water would pour over the southern bank, flowing west into the Caloosahatchee River and south into the Everglades, which extended down the peninsula 150 miles to the southern coast.

The Everglades region is saucer-shaped; the deepest part lies in the center, with the sides rising gently to form a rim. Incoming water moves toward the center, often keeping it flooded. The saucer tips gently toward the Gulf of Mexico, dropping about fifteen feet from north to south and sending the water slowly across the Everglades in a vast, shallow sheet some forty miles wide. It is this natural drainage that created the Everglades, a thirty-five-hundred-square-mile marsh dominated by sawgrass, a species with blades as long and as pointed as swords.

Today nearly fourteen hundred miles of canals direct the flow of Everglades water, and engineers have connected virtually all southern Florida's rivers and streams into the canal system. Now water flows from Lake Okeechobee into the Everglades only when the water manager of southern Florida wants it to. The Everglades as a natural ecosystem is dying, and some would say it is already dead.

But the destruction of the Everglades has not been easy. It required the concerted effort of state and federal bureaucracies and decades of determination. Within twenty years after Broward had scooped up the first shovelful of muck, the Everglades Drainage District had dredged 440 miles of canals, including five large ones for draining water into the Atlantic. It also had built forty-seven miles of levees and sixteen locks and thrown up a dike around Lake Okeechobee's southern edge, over which water had previously flowed into the Everglades. By the late 1940s, most of the major drainage works in use today were in place. In 1949, Congress created the Central and Southern Florida Project, which controlled water movement across 16,000 square miles, including 1,340 square miles of conservation flood pools that protected urban areas on the eastern—Everglades—side of the state.

Ironically, only two years before that, in 1947, Congress set aside the southern end of the Everglades as a national park, meant not to protect scenic splendor, as most national parks are, but specifically to protect the ecosystem and its wilderness values. The legislation creating it said the park "shall be permanently reserved as a wilderness and no development of the project or plan for the entertainment of visitors should be undertaken which will interfere with the preservation, intact, of the unique flora and fauna and essential primitive natural conditions now prevailing in the area."

Today, the park's 1.4 million acres make it our second-largest national park—only Yellowstone, at 2 million acres, is larger. But despite its size, the Everglades park has been severely affected by activities outside its borders. The many canals, locks, and other control structures in the more northern sections of the Everglades have shut down natural water flow into the park. During dry months, when water is most needed in the Everglades, state water managers have traditionally held back the flow. But when heavy rains came and the Everglades least needed water, the managers would open the gates of their overfilled reservoirs and flood the marsh to unnatural depths. This has caused widespread declines in wildlife, particularly bird species, which were not adapted to the conditions created by the new water flows.

Water flow is not the only problem. The park encloses only about 16 percent of the historic Everglades ecosystem. Agriculture has claimed about 25 percent of the ecosystem, water conservation areas about 30 percent, and other purposes—such as drainage—take what is left. These uses have ruined the quality of Everglades water. For example, farmers have converted 700,000 acres of marsh south of Lake Okeechobee into croplands, primarily sugarcane fields and dairy farms, which dominate the area around the lake. During the rainy season, runoff from these agricultural lands brings pesticides, fertilizers, and other pollutants into the Everglades system, and eventually into the national park, the last large stretch of undeveloped Everglades.

Gary Hendrix, the park research director, says: "I think one of the important things to realize about Everglades National Park is that it's only a piece of the larger Everglades system. Unfortunately, the park was established at the bottom of the Everglades system, so that the water that comes to it must come from above the park. The park is at the end of the river, at the end of the pipeline, and that makes it very difficult for us to manage our own destinies." Or, as Pat Tolle of Everglades National Park's public affairs office succinctly puts it, protecting the park "is like trying to restore a natural area in a sewer."

A look at the water pollutants coming into the park shows exactly what Tolle means. From farms come a variety of chemical and organic fertilizers that promote algal and other vegetative growth in Lake Okeechobee. This burst of plant growth can lead to a warming of surface waters and to a loss of dissolved oxygen, particularly as the plants die and decay. Although seemingly minor, these changes can destroy the aquatic ecosystem's food base.

Farm fertilizers—particularly phosphorus, a potent fertilizer that enters the park at nearly ten times the natural background rate—have converted nearly 40,000 acres of sawgrass Everglades into a cattail marsh, a different form of habitat in which some sawgrass-marsh species cannot survive. Even though the national park is sixty miles south of intensively agricultural areas, water-quality monitoring stations in the park have detected phosphorus at levels that result in harmful changes to the algae that form the food base for the Everglades ecosystem.

Nitrates, another form of pollutant that comes primarily from fertilizers, also seep into the park at alarmingly high levels. Found at 10 parts per billion in unaffected marshes, nitrates occur in affected park waters at 96 parts per billion—nearly ten times the background concentration. This can cause changes in plant growth that undermine the biological workings of the park.

South Florida also suffers the nation's highest levels of widespread mercury pollution, affecting some 2 million acres of freshwater systems. Although a state task force has been unable to locate a point source for the mercury, likely sources include such agricultural origins as cropland runoff and the yearly burning of sugarcane before harvest, which may release mercury trapped in cane tissues. Another possi-

ble source is the settling to earth of mercury from incinerator smokestacks. Every year, Florida garbage incinerators and power plants send about twenty-two thousand pounds of mercury into the atmosphere, enough on an average day to contaminate Niagara Falls six times over.

How deeply these ecological changes have affected the Everglades is reflected in the declining status of the animals that live there.

In the 1870s, an estimated 2.5 million wading birds nested in south Florida—primarily snowy egrets, great egrets, great blue herons, wood storks, white ibis, tricolored herons, and little blue herons. Today, 90 to 95 percent of them have disappeared. Between 1975 and 1989, the white ibis population shrank from nearly 12,000 pairs to only 1,600; the wood stork fell from 1,235 to 515 pairs; the great egret declined from nearly 3,000 pairs to fewer than 1,900; the snowy egret decreased from 4,474 to 506 pairs; and the tricolored heron from 2,900 to 650 pairs. The roseate spoonbill population

A great egret in Florida's "Ding" Darling National Wildlife Refuge seeks a perch after bathing. Populations of egrets, herons, storks and many other wading birds in the Sunshine State have declined—some drastically—in recent years.

A wood stork lands in a south Florida nesting colony. Populations of this species declined by more than half between 1975 and 1989, and the stork has been listed as endangered since 1984. Manipulation of water flows around the Everglades is largely to blame.

has decreased 50 percent since 1980. The Everglades kite dropped from 668 birds in 1984 to 418 in 1991, apparently because of changes in water flow that affected the kite's ability to obtain its primary food source, the apple snail. The decline of these species is a sign of profound disruption in the park and in the Everglades ecosystem itself.

The wood stork perhaps best shows how changes in water flow can affect fish-eating birds. Federally listed as endangered since 1984, the wood stork is the largest of the long-legged wading birds native to the United States. It stands between 5 and 5.5 feet tall and soars on wings spanning an equal length. The wood stork's plumage is white except for a short black tail and glossy black wing feathers. In young birds, the head and neck are feathered, but in adults they are naked and dark gray or blackish. Its large, heavy bill tapers to a point, the perfect weapon for capturing fish, which make up a large part of its diet.

A social bird that nests in colonies, the wood stork lives principally in wetlands across the southern United States, from South Carolina to southern California, also ranging south into central Argentina. Although the stork nests in all the Southern coastal states, its largest and most consistently used nesting sites lie in Florida. The nesting colonies, called rookeries, can number from a few nests to thousands. The storks sometimes share their rookeries with other large birds, such as herons, pelicans, and egrets. From a distance, the white storks look like myriad white blossoms in the green crowns of the trees. During the day a rookery seems in constant motion as storks feed their young or soar overhead, spiraling on outstretched wings.

The wood stork feeds almost entirely on fish, which it locates by probing with a partially opened bill in shallow water. When it touches a fish, a split-second reflex snaps the bill shut. In southern Florida, the stork nests during the winter dry season. As the sheet of water that inundates the Everglades during the rainy season dries or drains away, it breaks into small pools in low spots. The storks land in the pools, and dunking their featherless gray heads into the water, feel for fish. Because the fish are concentrated in the pools, the storks find ample food for their young.

To succeed in this style of hunting, the stork requires dense concentrations of fish. Optimal feeding conditions are found more often in undisturbed wetlands than in those altered by humans. As a result, environmental changes that reduce fish densities usually prove more harmful to the stork than to more generalized hunters such as herons and egrets, which feed on mollusks, amphibians, and other animals in addition to fish. Because the stork's fate is so intimately tied to wetlands ecosystems, its numbers and survival indicate the ecological health of its habitat. A decline in wood stork numbers is therefore quite likely a sign that the bird's homeland is in trouble.

Under natural conditions the stork's feeding system works well in most years. However, Florida water managers do not plan their releases of water around the needs of wood storks, so conditions are anything but natural. The birds in recent years often have been unable to nest because perpetually deep water prevents the trapping of fish in pools. This has resulted in a serious decline in the stork population. In the 1930s, estimates put stork numbers at sixty thousand in southern Florida, a population that may already have been reduced by the cumulative effects of cypress logging and a miscellany of other human-caused disturbances, such as canalization. Between the early 1930s and the late 1950s, the U.S. stork population fell by half. This alarming development led the National Audubon Society, the Florida Audubon Society, and the Florida Game and Fresh Water Fish Commission to initiate stork surveys in the 1960s that indicated that only twenty thousand of these birds survived in southern Florida.

Since then, the trend in stork numbers has been generally downward. This was sometimes masked because wood storks' nesting success, for unknown reasons, varied from year to year, with an occasional bumper crop of chicks punctuating a long series of low years, giving the impression that the bird was recovering. The apparent overall decline, however, stimulated the National Audubon Society in the 1970s to undertake annual aerial surveys of all U.S. stork rookeries. The surveys showed a decline of 52 percent in stork numbers nationwide between 1960 and 1980, with a decline of 75

A month-old panther plays in the south Florida underbrush. Mercury poisoning from several sources has been implicated in the deaths of at least three endangered Florida panthers, including the last known females in Everglades National Park. (facing page)

percent in southern Florida. In 1985, only 30 percent of the nesting storks counted in 1970 remained. Since then, despite good nesting years, such as occurred in 1992, the stork population has continued to dwindle.

The declines in southern Florida represent both an actual drop in the number of surviving birds and a movement of the birds to other areas. As the Everglades have become increasingly difficult for storks to live in, some of the birds have moved northward, and others have shifted to artificial reservoirs or have moved from inland to coastal sites. Unfortunately, this apparent sign of adaptation on the part of individual storks does not truly indicate success for the species as a whole. For millions of years the Everglades has offered the wood stork the best nesting sites, and when forced to abandon these areas, the stork has no choice but to move to less suitable, poorer rookeries. Living in less than ideal habitats, the surviving populations become increasingly vulnerable to disruptions such as harsh weather or lean feeding seasons. John Ogden, a biologist with the Everglades National Park, says, "The fact that the wood storks [would] abandon the areas that were the heart of their range and move into these areas that were at one time the edge of their breeding range, the marginal areas, certainly is a powerful message that the Everglades themselves have changed dramatically, drastically, have changed for the worse in their ability to support these birds in these last ten or twenty years."

Another Everglades denizen that shows the effects of human intrusion on the area is the endangered Florida panther. The last surviving subspecies of cougar native to the Eastern United States, the Florida panther probably numbers no more than fifty animals, all living in southern Florida. In 1991 biologists found that a male panther that had died from no immediately apparent cause was carrying 110 parts per million of mercury in his liver—roughly 75 times the 1.5 parts per million that the federal government believes is the maximum safe level for humans. The mercury was a likely contributor to and perhaps the cause of the cat's death. He probably ingested it by eating raccoons, which pick up mercury by eating contaminated fish and other aquatic organisms.

In June 1991, a female panther found dead in the park had 35 parts per million of mercury in her liver and 15 parts per million in her blood. Biologists suspected that mercury also caused the death of another female found dead one month later. These were the park's last remaining female panthers.

Others species also bear unhealthy mercury levels. Biologists have discovered such high levels of mercury in alligators from Everglades conservation areas that in recent years planned hunts were shut down. Soft-shelled turtles and a variety of wading birds have shown dangerously high levels of mercury. In early 1989, the Florida Department of Environmental Regulation reported that mercury levels in fish from water conservation areas north of the park stood at about 1.5 parts per million. Later in 1989, park officials, with the assistance of the U.S. Fish and Wildlife Service and the Florida Department of Health and Rehabilitative Services, found high levels of mercury in fish from six freshwater locations in the park, and park administrators immediately created no-consumption or limited-consumption fishing zones in those waters.

While the problems that beset the Everglades are remarkable, they are not unique. In many states, little of the original wetlands remains. Ninety-five percent of California's Central Valley wetlands are gone. So are 95 percent of Iowa's wetlands, although the recent Missouri River flood suggests that nature will make periodic attempts to reclaim these lowlands. Minnesota has lost more than 90 percent of its marshes and swamps, and North Dakota—the heart of the prairie pothole (pond) country that produces 80 percent of the ducks bred in the lower forty-eight states—has lost half its wetlands. Canada, too, has suffered losses—40 percent of total wetlands in Alberta, Saskatchewan, and Manitoba, all prime waterfowl country, are gone. About 90 percent of the wetlands lost from the mid-1950s to the mid-1970s were drained for agriculture.

This shrinking of wetlands has far-reaching effects on the wildlife community. Many duck populations, including those of mallards, blue-winged teal, and pintails, are 20 to 50 percent below the average level of the past thirty-five years. Examination of specific wetlands sites suggests why waterfowl as well as other bird species dependent upon wetlands are dwindling.

Kesterson National Wildlife Refuge lies in California's Central Valley, which runs down the middle of the state. The valley attracts twelve million waterfowl every winter, about 60 percent of all ducks and geese that migrate along the Pacific Coast. Most of the water that fills Kesterson's wetlands comes from nearby farms. In the early 1980s, biologists discovered that toxic minerals, notably a salt called selenium, that occur naturally in local soils but become concentrated in agricultural runoff were causing widespread birth defects among birds nesting in Kesterson, signaling a possible threat to nearby human residents. In recent years, the U.S. Fish and Wildlife Service, which runs the refuge, has tried to keep birds out of Kesterson, which ironically was set aside for waterfowl in the first place. The federal Bureau of Reclamation recently agreed to provide refuges with more water from federal reservoirs, offering hope for beleaguered waterfowl.

The Louisiana Delta, a vast wetland surrounding the mouth of the Mississippi River, has served since time immemorial as a wintering ground for millions of ducks, geese, and other waterbirds. The marsh is founded on silt washed into the area by the Mississippi from northern sites. Today, because oil developers have crisscrossed the area with canals and upstream dams have altered river flow, the silt is washing away. In the past quarter century, 750,000 acres of Louisiana marsh have disappeared. Southern Louisiana loses fifty square miles of freshwater marshes yearly to incoming salt water from the Gulf of Mexico.

North and South Dakota have lost half their prairie potholes—the small ponds heavily used by breeding ducks—since 1960. As ducks have been restricted to smaller ponds and poorer habitat, they have succumbed increasingly to predators. In the 1950s, coyotes, foxes, crows, and other animals destroyed perhaps half of all waterfowl nests; now they have taken up to 90 percent. To stem this destruction, waterfowl managers have initiated control programs, killing the predators and further disrupting the ecosystem.

Delaware Bay, lying between New Jersey and Delaware, is the most critical resting spot for shorebirds traveling the Atlantic Coast during their northward migration from Latin America to the Arctic. Although the birds still gather by the hundreds of thousands in spring, pollution and coastal development have seriously damaged the bay and the birds. As a result, the number of migrating birds has dropped steadily since the mid-1970s.

The twenty-five thousand acres comprising Stillwater National Wildlife Refuge, east of Reno, Nevada, include marshlands that have long been home to the largest white pelican nesting colony in North America. Presently, however, birds are dying in many parts of the marsh. Analyses of bird tissues show that the animals are contaminated with natural soil toxins, such as arsenic, boron, and selenium, that build up in agricultural runoff. Diversion of water for irrigation is also shrinking the marsh, which is vital to migrating shorebirds, including avocets, black-necked stilts, curlews, dowitchers, and various sandpipers. Studies of other national wildlife refuges have revealed that similar problems exist throughout the agricultural West.

Cheyenne Bottoms, once a vast wetlands in central Kansas that was used by migrating waterfowl, is now often dry because the rivers and other water sources that fed it have been diverted for irrigation. As waterfowl coming to the area are concentrated into fewer and smaller wetlands, they become increasingly susceptible to contagious diseases, such as the avian cholera that killed nearly 100,000 waterfowl in Nebraska's Rainwater Basin in 1980.

These and many similar situations tell us that wetlands loss and degradation are jeopardizing myriad species, putting the wetlands themselves in trouble. Nevertheless, some cause for hope does exist. Ironically, it lies in the Everglades, one of the most damaged of all wetlands ecosystems.

While ecological degradation often seems so widespread that any protective effort seems futile, the conditions that degrade the environment can be changed if society has the will to do it. One place where that will seems to exist is Florida, where the Save Our Everglades project initiated by

Senator Bob Graham when he was governor in the early 1980s promises to undo many of the developments that fragmented southern Florida. It will create water flows similar to those found under natural conditions and initiate a management plan for the entire Everglades ecosystem. It will even seek to reverse old Army Corps of Engineer projects that have wrought havoc on the Everglades. Under the Save Our Everglades program, the Corps will attempt to restore as much as possible the original course of the Kissimmee River, straightened long ago by a channelization project. The Corps will also cut openings in a canal that crosses a large marsh north of Everglades National Park and elevate parts of U.S. Highway 41 to permit water flow and animal traffic beneath it. Water from the canal will flow across both the park and a newly acquired 107,000-acre addition. These attempts to restore a more natural water regimen will keep the park from drying out in winter and drowning in rainy summers. In addition, in a drive to reduce mercury pollution, the State of Florida has initiated a program that will cut mercury effluents from waste incinerators by as much as 80 percent.

When Graham first started the Save Our Everglades program, he said the goal was to restore the southern end of Florida to a condition more like that of 1900 than that of the present. But plans for the Everglades do not stop there. Florida officials and The Nature Conservancy are attempting to locate and purchase the state's largest remaining blocks of essentially unbroken wildland in order to create a string of large protected areas with a natural or nearly natural diversity of species. Strips or corridors of wildland will be added to these to connect the larger areas into one long system. Wildlands along rivers and streams will probably be the most common corridors because they tend to be deeply wooded and are frequently traveled by large mammals, such as the Florida panther. The state has been investing about $100 million yearly to build the network, which ultimately could run from the Everglades to Georgia. The effort is massive and in many ways unprecedented. Senator Graham explains why it is worthwhile: "The Everglades are part of what south Florida is. It would be like the Rocky Mountains and their relationship to the state of Colorado. If we lost our

Everglades, we would not only be losing a resource, we would be losing our individuality, our character, our specialness."

Although developments such as the Save Our Everglades project give cause for encouragement, hope for the future must be tempered with political realism. In attempting to deal with the Everglades, the federal and state governments have tended to placate powerful local agricultural interests. Citrus farming is Florida's number one industry after tourism, bringing in $2 billion yearly. Florida's sugar industry annually produces more than 13 million tons of cane, which is refined into 100 million gallons of blackstrap molasses and 1.5 million tons of sugar, a quarter of the nation's sugar production. This represents a great deal of wealth and a great many jobs—the yearly payroll for the Florida sugar industry stands at about $200 million. That money buys a lot of political influence, and the agricultural industry has ensured that no program designed to save the Everglades will become an obstacle to its use of fertilizers.

Will the Everglades recover under the new regimen? Only time will tell. To date, agricultural interests have consistently thwarted attempts to initiate altered water regimens and land use.

Some promise for wetlands across the nation exists in the federal government, which under President Clinton is seeking to revise national wetlands management. The Clinton administration announced its new plan in the summer of 1993. One goal of the program is to ensure that the nation suffers no further net loss of wetlands, which sounds ambitious, given that the United States loses about 300,000 acres of wetlands to development—mostly agricultural—every year. The problematic aspect of this goal is the wording. "No net loss of wetlands" does not necessarily mean that wetlands will be protected from destruction. It can mean that if a swamp or marsh is drained or in some other way destroyed, developers can mitigate, or make up for, the loss by building a new swamp or marsh elsewhere. The idea of mitigation has propped up wetlands destruction for decades. Unfortunately, it has never worked. No scientific evidence has been mustered to prove that an artificial wetland can replace a real one. While an artificial wetland may look like a natural one, no data exist to show that it will function like a natural one or provide habitat to the same species of plants and animals. Moreover, mitigation does not guarantee that a lost wetland will be replaced by the same type of wetland. For example, a swamp, dominated by trees, may be replaced by a marsh, dominated by grasses. Nevertheless, the Clinton administration has emphasized mitigation as a wetlands protection measure.

Will the future brighten for wetlands? That will depend less upon the politicians in office than upon the people who vote for them. Even the Clinton administration, more environmentally oriented than most, is weak on many environmental issues. Only strong constituent support for wetlands protection, and other environmentally sound programs, can win political action. If voters do not in their multitudes speak loudly, their voices will be drowned out by those of powerful forces such as the Florida sugar industry.

Chapter Eight

THE AIR WE BREATHE

As we breathe, air filters through our lungs and into our bloodstream, bringing into our bodies many chemicals that we as humans are responsible for putting into the air—oxides of nitrogen and sulfur, heavy metals, pesticides, particulate matter, and a host of other toxins. Today, nearly 70 percent of U.S. residents live in areas that exceed pollution levels declared safe by the federal government.

One atmospheric contaminant is carbon monoxide, an odorless toxic gas that comes from the incomplete burning of fossil fuels and that can block or reduce the body's ability to absorb oxygen, leading to fatigue, headache, even death. Other contaminants include the pollutants that make up smog. These include many volatile, carbon-containing compounds found in fossil fuels and industrial chemicals. Once they enter the atmosphere, sunlight and heat transform them into hazardous compounds. Ozone and nitrogen oxides, both by-products of fossil fuel combustion, also add to the smog in our atmosphere.

Sulfur dioxides, produced when coal or other fossil fuels with a high sulfur content are burned, are another major cause of air pollution. Once in the atmosphere, sulfur dioxides undergo changes that make them acidic. The acid precipitation that results proves deadly to many lakes and trees around the globe.

In addition to these pollutants, the air contains many toxic chemicals that are used in a wide variety of industrial processes, such as oil refining. In all, human society releases about seventy thousand different chemical contaminants into the atmosphere each year.

A final major cause of air pollution is particulate matter, which includes liquid droplets and particles of soot, dust, and ash that waft through the air and are small enough to be inhaled. A Harvard University study released in 1993 con-

A blanket of smog covers Los Angeles. The outlook on clean air is not reassuring in most major cities, few of which are in compliance with EPA air-quality standards. Global warming of just a few degrees would intensify the health risks posed by polluted metropolitan air. (facing page)

cluded that about sixty thousand human deaths result each year from particulate pollution.

Of course, the danger presented by *all* forms of air pollution is illness and death. Carbon monoxide inhaled by a pregnant woman may threaten the growth and mental development of her child. Lead has been linked to decreased learning ability and hyperactivity in children. Ozone can double allergic sensitivity in people with asthma. Nitrogen oxides may lower resistance to some viral infections and contribute to bronchitis. An increasing body of evidence links toxic chemicals to cancer and various reproductive problems, including birth defects.

Air pollution also harms wildlife and its environments. Acid rain has eliminated fish from 13,000 square kilometers of fresh water in Norway. It has rendered 2,200 Swedish lakes nearly lifeless and another 14,000 unable to support sensitive aquatic life. Some biologists suspect that acid precipitation is the underlying cause of reductions in many amphibian populations around the globe. Scientists have linked ozone pollution to declines in ponderosa and Jeffrey pines in California. A 1987 federal report prepared by the National Acid Precipitation Assessment Program concluded that ozone pollution reduces U.S. crop production by 5 to 10 percent yearly, an annual loss of nearly $6 billion. For alfalfa, the annual crop reduction is as high as 30 percent.

The Environmental Protection Agency, created in 1970, is the primary federal agency responsible for regulating air pollution. Unfortunately, since the EPA's inception, certain factors have limited its effectiveness in enforcing the pollution restrictions outlined in the Clean Air Act. One major obstacle lies in the difficulty of proving links between specific pollutants and their effects on health. Although probable correlations can be found, humans are exposed to so many chemicals and external influences each day that it is nearly scientifically impossible to isolate one single factor as causing a specific negative effect.

In addition, industrial interests have sought to place obstacles in the way of regulation. Automobile manufacturers maintained that they would go out of business when in the 1970s the EPA ordered them to reduce the lead emissions of their vehicles by 90 percent. The auto industry launched a campaign to block the regulations, saying the goal was too costly and, in any event, impossible to achieve. In this case, the industy's effort failed. Subsequently, automakers set to work developing cleaner cars. As a result, today's cars produce 96 percent less lead than did cars in 1970.

Although the industrial community continues to fight environmental regulation, the battle flies in the face of popular sentiment. In 1993, the Opinion Research Corporation conducted a survey that showed that while only 44 percent of business executives place a priority on environmental cleanup, 74 percent of the public does. Nearly 70 percent of the public said the government spends too little on environmental cleanup; only 45 percent of executives agreed. A *Times-Mirror* poll found that 68 percent of Americans believe environmental protection and economic development can go hand in hand, and 59 percent said that when it is impossible to find a reasonable compromise between environmental protection and economic development, protection should take precedence. This public support for a healthier environment could, if it became vocal, translate into stronger implementation of national environmental laws, including regulations for cleaner air.

Despite sometimes lackadaisical implementation of national clean-air regulations, in the two decades that have followed passage of the federal Clean Air Act some measures of air quality have improved. These include a drop in Los Angeles's ground-level ozone to fifteen-year lows. (Although ozone is a critical sunscreen when it occurs high in the atmosphere, it is a dangerous pollutant at ground level.) Smog warnings issued in major American cities such as Los Angeles, New York, Washington, D.C., and Philadelphia dropped by 50 percent between 1988 and 1993. Between 1982 and 1992, ozone pollution declined 8 percent, carbon monoxide pollution 30 percent, and airborne lead 89 percent nationwide. During the same period, in sites tested by the U.S. Geological Survey, airborne sulfur dioxide declined by 20 percent, with a concomitant decline in the acidity of rain. In 1987, Congress enacted a law requiring corporations to disclose their emissions of 320 chemicals. Since then, emissions of these chemicals have dropped 31 percent. Early in 1994, the EPA issued regulations requiring disclosure of emissions of an additional 300 chemicals.

Depletion of the ozone layer seems to be slowing in the wake of reductions in the use of ozone-destroying chemicals called chlorofluorocarbons (CFCs). Use of CFCs as propellants in aerosol cans was discontinued in the 1970s, but the chemicals are still widely used as coolants in air conditioners and refrigerators. When released into the air, often as the result of leakage, the compounds rise about fifteen miles to the atmospheric ozone layer, which blocks deadly ultraviolet rays from the sun. Once in the ozone layer, the CFCs undergo chemical reactions that destroy ozone molecules, thinning the layer and reducing its ability to block ultraviolet light.

Each summer, when atmospheric conditions facilitate the chemical reactions leading to ozone depletion, the ozone layer wears especially thin over the Antarctic and surrounding areas. Residents of New Zealand and Australia, areas that already receive long hours of summer sun, are especially concerned because of the increased potential for skin cancer from ultraviolet exposure. Evidence of ozone thinning in the Northern Hemisphere has also grown in recent years. Researchers reported the first known incident of ozone-layer thinning over the United States in 1991.

But a solution to the problem is in sight. The chemical

Chlorofluorocarbons (CFCs) in air conditioners, refrigerators, and other products are prime destroyers of stratospheric ozone. Use of CFCs should be phased out by the year 2000, but existing molecules in the atmosphere will continue to "eat" ozone for several decades.

industry is rapidly developing new coolants that will not harm the ozone layer, and some companies have already cut down the production of CFCs and other ozone-damaging chemicals. CFC reduction carries international implications, since the chemicals cross national borders and produce problems on a global scope. Measurements taken in the 1990s suggest that the destruction of the ozone layer is slowing as the amount of CFCs in the atmosphere declines. If the trend continues, the layer could repair itself as early as the middle of the next century.

Although the United States has made some improvements in air quality, other parts of the globe still suffer from severe pollution, particularly in the developing world, where most motor vehicles lack catalytic converters for reducing exhaust pollutants, a large component of air pollution. According to the standards of the World Health Organization (WHO), the air in Mexico City was safe and breathable on only thirty-one days in 1993. In a 1988 study, 70 percent of newborn babies in Mexico City showed blood lead levels that exceeded WHO standards. And the United States, despite national gains, continues to contribute to global air pollution. The United States is the world's number one producer of carbon dioxide, accounting for 25 percent of worldwide emissions of the gas, a leading component in perhaps the greatest air pollution problem of all, global warming.

Global warming is a product of the greenhouse effect, the trapping of the sun's heat close to the surface of the globe by atmospheric gases. These gases act much as does the glass exterior of a greenhouse, keeping solar heat from radiating back into space. Under natural conditions, this effect is beneficial; it keeps the Earth at temperatures hospitable to life as we know it. But the greenhouse effect is no longer functioning under normal conditions. Instead, gases released by human activities—anthropogenic gases—may be heightening the effect and causing the globe to warm at a speed that can result in extensive biological, social, and economic damage.

Chief among the anthropogenic gases that augment the greenhouse effect is carbon dioxide. It accounts for half of the atmospheric gases that are likely to raise global temperatures in the next fifty years. Each year, global burning of fossil fuels adds nearly 6 billion tons of carbon dioxide to the atmosphere. Approximately 2 billion additional tons comes from the burning and clearing of forests. Although the oceans and various terrestrial organisms absorb more than half of this, a net gain of 3 billion tons of carbon is added to the atmosphere each year. Since 1860, 175 billion tons of anthropogenic carbon has entered the atmosphere, most of it since World War II.

Another greenhouse gas, methane, produced when wood is burned and when fossil fuels are extracted, accounts for 20 percent of greenhouse gases. Chlorofluorocarbons—used as air-conditioner refrigerants, and the leading culprits in the destruction of the Earth's protective ozone layer—account for 15 percent of greenhouse gases. The remaining 15 percent is composed of nitrous oxides, derived from sources including chemical fertilizers that have broken down and burning coal; and ground-based ozone, which is produced by petrochemical refineries, fossil fuel-powered motor vehicles, and power plants.

Between 1960 and 1990—a period during which greenhouse gases rapidly increased in the atmosphere—the average global temperature warmed by a full degree, yielding the highest mean global temperature since record keeping began 130 years ago. Various mathematical models designed to predict the extent of global warming have run data such as these through sophisticated computer programs—some taking as long as ten hours to compute one year of weather— and all generally predict that a doubling of the Earth's atmospheric carbon dioxide will raise average global temperatures two to ten degrees during the next century. The likelihood that these models are correct is about 50 percent.

The last time the Earth warmed by that magnitude was about twelve thousand years ago, when average global temperatures rose nine degrees. That rise ended a hundred-thousand-year ice age and melted the mile-high glaciers that had covered large expanses of the Northern Hemisphere. By the time the warming trend stabilized, many large mammals were lost—woolly mammoths, woolly rhinos, giant sloths, and cave bears. The birch tree vanished from Europe. Ecological zones shifted. The world turned into the one humanity has known for the past ten thousand years, the one to which we and all our agriculture and livestock are adapted.

For some people, the idea that the Earth stands a 50 percent chance of warming does not seem impressive. The Bush administration, for example, consistently rebuffed international efforts to reduce global carbon dioxide emissions. But many scientists consider this a high percentage in a dangerous game, especially since the computer models that predict the extent of global warming are as likely to be wrong on the high end as on the low.

Everybody talks about the weather, but nobody does anything about it—or so Charles Dudley Warner declared in an editorial in the *Hartford Courant* on August 24, 1897. Ironically, even as those words were being written something was being done about the weather, and someone had taken note of it only a year before.

That individual was a Swedish physicist and chemist named Svante Arrhenius. As he watched his nation's march down the path of industrialism late in the 1800s, his attention was drawn to industrial effluents. He predicted that a doubling of carbon dioxide in the atmosphere would increase average global temperatures by nine to eleven degrees, with the greatest shift occurring at higher altitudes.

Although Arrhenius won a Nobel Prize in 1903 for his work in chemistry, his ideas about global warming were not well received in the scientific world and were essentially ignored for the next sixty years. History has justified him, though: His predictions have proved correct. Evidence of this began to accumulate in 1957, when two scientists with the Scripps Institution of Oceanography published a paper in the journal *Tellus* in which they discussed the absorption of carbon dioxide by oceans. They speculated that humanity was putting carbon dioxide into the atmosphere faster than the oceans could absorb it and that consequently, carbon dioxide was accumulating in the air. This, they suggested, could lead to unanticipated shifts in climate.

One author of the *Tellus* paper, Roger Revelle, was the director of Scripps. He commissioned a young scientist named Charles Keeling to undertake a study that would determine whether carbon dioxide was building up in the atmosphere. Keeling started measuring atmospheric carbon dioxide in 1958 at the South Pole and at the Mauna Loa Observatory on a Hawaiian mountaintop. The data, still being collected, show that atmospheric carbon dioxide has increased 11 percent since the research began.

Although some argue that the increased carbon dioxide comes from natural sources—including volcanic eruptions, digestive gases emitted by animals, evaporation of water, chemical processes in wetlands, and the decay of dead organic matter—and that the current increase is part of a natural cycle, recent research tends to disprove this theory. Analysis of air pockets that have been trapped in Antarctic ice for thousands of years shows that the highest concentration of atmospheric carbon dioxide during the past 160,000 years is occurring right now—355 parts per million. Today's levels are also significantly higher than any previous peaks, indicating that even with the occurrence of natural cycles, additional factors have contributed to the recent rise. These can be attributed to only one cause: human activity.

It is, of course, practically impossible to predict with certainty just what climatic changes will occur if the planet's mean annual temperatures rise. However, the bulk of scientific evidence suggests that the globe will warm by a greater percentage than has occurred since the last ice age. This was the conclusion reached in a report from the Intergovernmental Panel on Climate Change, established in 1988 by the United Nations General Assembly to advise international leaders on global warming. The report, signed by three hundred scientists, declared that "emissions resulting from human activities are substantially increasing the atmospheric concentrations of the greenhouse gases. . . . These increases will enhance the greenhouse effect, resulting on average in an additional warming of the Earth's surface." Because a change of such magnitude cannot fail to have far-reaching effects, forty-nine Nobel laureates sent a more pointed message to President Bush in 1990 urging him to take action because "global warming has emerged as the most serious environmental threat of the twenty-first century."

If warming does occur, it is possible that the Earth's poles will heat up three times more than the mean temperature change—as much as thirty degrees. Ice will melt. The Arctic, a frozen sea with no land beneath it, may vanish before the end of the twenty-first century. Global warming could result in as much as a six-foot rise in sea levels because as the oceans warm they will expand, as any object expands when heated. The addition of melted polar ice will contribute to a sea rise that will probably threaten Indonesia, Pakistan, Thailand, and Bangladesh. England will lose much of its coastal zone. In the Netherlands, the likelihood that the famous dikes will be overrun will increase from once every ten thousand years to once every one hundred. Among the most vulnerable cities are those on Mediterranean shores. The citizens of Venice are already threatened, as are the 3.5 million residents of Alexandria, Egypt, most of whom live on land less than three feet above sea level. The wetlands of southern France will be inundated. U.S. cities vulnerable to flooding include New York, Boston, Miami, New Orleans, Los Angeles, and San Francisco. Water supplies will become polluted as sea levels rise, inundating sources of fresh water, such as coastal rivers, with salt water.

Coastal wetlands, which are important breeding areas and nurseries for many commercial marine fish species, will be lost throughout the world. A five-foot rise in sea level would flood about one-third of all U.S. coastal wetlands; a seven-foot rise could destroy two-thirds nationally. If coastal wetlands disappear at rates such as these, the nation will lose as much as 70 percent of its $5.5-billion commercial coastal fishing industry as fish breeding areas are ruined. Of course, many other wild creatures and their habitats will also suffer from the widespread effects of global warming.

People, too, will feel the impact as the planet's climate changes. One effect will be the heightening of global temperatures, particularly in the summer. In the mid-twentieth century, unusually hot summers occurred about once every three years. Through the 1990s, that occurrence will probably double to twice every three years. By 2010, the Earth will be warmer than it has been for more than one hundred thousand years. What once was an abnormally hot summer will become the norm. This is already becoming apparent. Since

1980, the world has endured six of the seven hottest years on record. And rising temperatures will not be the sole problem. Storms will become more severe, including more winter blizzards and summer droughts in the United States and Europe, as well as more severe hurricanes. Crop production may decline in many places around the globe, including the United States, where almost the entire nation will be considerably drier after atmospheric carbon dioxide doubles. In the bread basket of the United States, an increase in temperature of four degrees will reduce grain production by as much as 17 percent. As rainfall drops, droughts could prevail. Some parts of the globe will probably receive less rain, but average global rainfall will very likely increase because water evaporates more quickly in warmer weather. Greater rainfall is particularly likely in the higher latitudes. Continental interiors in the middle latitudes will most likely become drier and warmer.

A study conducted in the late 1980s in New York City found that when summer temperatures rise above ninety-two degrees, deaths from heat exposure increase. Heat intensifies reactions to problems such as cardiovascular, respiratory, and cerebrovascular diseases, particularly among the sick, the elderly, and the very young. If atmospheric carbon dioxide doubles, as has been predicted, and brings concomitant rises in mean global temperatures, heat-related deaths in the United States will probably double, presuming that people become acclimated to the higher temperatures. However, wider use of air-conditioning may keep many people from fully acclimating, so heat-related mortality could multiply an estimated six times, with most deaths occurring among the elderly.

Hay fever and other respiratory problems will probably also increase and intensify, and various diseases limited to the tropics and other warm areas are likely to move into new regions. Among these are parasitic diseases such as amebiasis, hookworm, schistosomiasis, trypanosomiasis, yellow fever, and dengue fever. New York, London, Paris, and Rome may become warm enough to support the mosquito that transmits malaria. Fungal diseases will probably become more severe as many climates grow more humid.

The planet has warmed before; it has also cooled off. Mean

temperatures were perhaps fifteen degrees warmer when dinosaurs roamed and eight or nine degrees cooler during the ice ages. Not all species survived these fluctuations, but enough did to ensure that life would continue.

What makes the present warming trend so alarming is not the mere fact of increased warmth. Under natural conditions, many species could adapt to that. The danger lies in the speed with which the change is occurring. The global warming that brought the most recent ice age to an end occurred at a fiftieth of the rate likely to occur today, yet even at that speed the planet lost many species, including thirty-two genera of mammals.

It is not clear exactly which species are most at risk. Certainly those that are least mobile, and therefore least able to move from warming areas, will be threatened. This includes many plant species. Organisms that reproduce slowly will also be at risk because it will take them longer to adapt to change. Insects, bacteria, and various microrganisms will be in a good position to survive because they pass quickly through several generations, giving them a better chance to adapt to warmer climates through natural selection.

Tropical rain forests may suffer drastically. According to some computer models, northern reaches of the Brazilian rain forest and much of Africa's rain forest will become drier in the next century. The rain forest's dependence upon abundant precipitation could doom large portions of these ecosystems even if they survive current cutting and burning.

The problem of survival is compounded for many species because humanity has swamped the globe. Under more natural conditions, animals at the northern end of their range might survive warming by shifting farther north, while individuals at the southern end of a species' range might be lost, unable to traverse heated expanses. But in a world dominated by people, wildlife species in most nations have become locked into small reserves isolated from one another by vast areas of development through which they cannot pass.

In areas prone to burning, such as the Great Plains, the increasingly dry climate may cause the incidence of fires to double. Oak, conifer, and chaparral regions are likely to become more incendiary as well. Wetlands are likely to disappear as coasts flood and rainfall declines in continental interiors, forcing migratory birds to concentrate at fewer and fewer rest stops. This biological stress will increase the likelihood of disease, and crowding will promote epidemics.

Even shifts in the ranges of disease organisms could have devastating effects on wild creatures and places. The tsetse fly, because it carries the organism that causes sleeping sickness, keeps people out of much of central Africa, where it is endemic. If the climate warms by four degrees, the fly could move south, vacating its present range and making the area habitable to people and subject to environmental destruction.

Global warming may prove the undoing of years of dedicated conservation work. One of the first victims of global warming may be the Kirtland's warbler, which nests in the jack pine plains of northeastern Michigan. The subject of strict protection since the 1930s, the species numbered about one thousand when surveyed in 1951. In the 1960s it sank to four hundred. An intensive management program by the U.S. Fish and Wildlife Service has stabilized the population at that number, but so far the number of birds has not increased. If atmospheric carbon dioxide levels double by the middle of the next century as predicted, the species may simply vanish. The warblers cannot survive without jack pines, and the pines cannot grow in higher temperatures. By 2070, the jack pine plains may be replaced with grasses and low shrubs, and the Kirtland's warbler may be extinct.

Another species painstakingly saved from oblivion by intensive management is the alligator, found in wetlands and along streams throughout the Deep South. Uncontrolled hunting for its hide nearly wiped out the alligator by the middle of the twentieth century, but strict protection has helped it to rebound. It has even been removed from the federal endangered and threatened species list in some states. But the success of alligator protection may be completely undermined by global warming because the sex of alligators is determined by the temperature at which the eggs are incubated. Alligator eggs incubated at ninety-two degrees or less become females. Those incubated at warmer temperatures become males. A shift of only two degrees in the alligators' habitat is enough to cause an entire nesting season to yield only males. Because alligators have fairly long lives—they may survive for sixty years or more—they may seem to thrive for many decades before the dying off of a virtually all-male populace begins.

Another possibility is that as warming trends develop, alligators at the northern end of their range may move farther northward as the higher latitudes become increasingly hospitable to them. If they can get past various dam and diversion projects, towns, and developments, and survive in polluted waters, alligators may someday nest in Illinois and along parts of the Ohio River.

Massive environmental shifts may also doom large numbers of creatures in one fell swoop. A good example of this can be found along Delaware Bay. Every May, when the moon has waned, tides in the bay area reach their peak. The warmth of the water and the height of the tides signal the horseshoe crabs of the region that it is time to come ashore and breed. Marine relatives of spiders, these ancient beasts have scuttled across the Earth for millions of years, a living memory of a lost, primordial world. For the past several hundred thousand years they have shared their nesting beaches with hundreds of thousands of migrating birds that feed on horseshoe crab eggs.

Pete Maclean, a biologist who for thirty-five years has helped to establish protected beaches in the Delaware Bay area for migrating birds, says: "This is the second largest concentration of spring migrating shorebirds in the Western Hemisphere. When they come up from Argentina, Brazil, Peru, Surinam, they key in on those migrating areas to stop to feed. They'll lose 50 percent of their body weight during the migration, and it's absolutely imperative to allow these birds to double that body weight, which they do in about fifteen days, to continue their migration to the high Canadian Arctic, which is another three thousand miles."

The birds crowd the beaches, moving among the horseshoe crabs, which cruise the shore like miniature tanks. The crabs' tiny, dark eggs look like soot on the sand, and the birds gorge on them. The birds' migration is synchronized to bring them to the beach during the two weeks when the horseshoe crabs are nesting. This is the only time when the

An alligator suns itself in Georgia's Okefenokee Swamp National Wildlife Refuge. Because the gender of their offspring is determined by temperatures during incubation, alligators are among the first species that would likely be affected by global warming.

birds will find the sustenance they need to continue their journey to northern nesting grounds.

The delicate balance between the birds' arrival and the horseshoe crabs' egg laying may be disrupted by global warming. If temperatures rise, the horseshoe crabs may finish breeding in April, a month before the birds appear. When the birds land in May, they will be greeted by empty sand rather than by the banquet that is crucial to their survival. Without the Delaware Bay feeding stop, perhaps 90 percent of the shorebirds, including species such as red knots and ruddy turnstones, would not make it to the Arctic breeding grounds.

Global warming could affect many invisible species as well. These are microscopic creatures that few think of in relation to global warming, but that nevertheless can have serious effects on ecological integrity. As soils warm, the activities of microorganisms will change. Bacteria may become more active, increasing the rate at which they decompose organic material, cycle nutrients through the soil, and produce gases. This may cause soil chemistry to change, and as a result, plants characteristic of certain regions may fail to survive. In the ancient forests of the Pacific Northwest trees grow that depend on the fungi that surround their roots for nutrients. If the soil chemistry alters, will the fungi survive? If the fungi vanish, will the trees with which they are associated disappear? Will the character of the ancient forests be lost?

It is unlikely that we can predict all the possible changes—from storm severity to soil chemistry, from loss of rainfall to increased heat—that global warming will bring to our environment. But by ignoring the problem, we are in effect playing dice with the entire planet. Or, to look at it another way: If the National Academy of Sciences sought funding for a research project designed to heat up the globe by ten degrees to see just what would happen, we would take one look at the possibilities and say forget it. No one would be willing to go through with an experiment like that. Too much is at stake. And yet here we are, watching it happen, while our government reacts lethargically.

Among us are some hardy souls, perhaps more trusting than insightful, who believe that technology can solve any prob-

Horseshoe crabs cluster at the shoreline of Delaware Bay in May. The coincidence of crab mating and shorebird migrations could easily be disrupted by changes in global temperatures. This could result in a sudden overpopulation of horseshoe crabs and an equally swift decimation of the birds.

lem. Such people say that if the globe warms, we will avoid the entire issue with some kind of fix-it solution. Some of the solutions that have been proposed are terrifically imaginative, but they are also highly impractical. One plan calls for putting huge satellites into space that would orbit the globe and cast a cooling shadow over it. Another calls for painting every rooftop white to reflect sunlight back into space.

A more realistic approach, and one that targets the cause of the problem and not the symptom, is to try to reduce the greenhouse gases pumped into the atmosphere. Figures prepared by the National Academy of Sciences suggest that reducing the use of fossil fuels and increasing the use of less polluting fuels and energy-efficient machinery could cost from $800 billion to $3.6 trillion between now and the year 2100. Those figures seem daunting, but broken down over the one-hundred-year period are not all that bad. Put into perspective, $8 billion dollars to $36 billion yearly is only a small fraction of the annual defense budget, which, until recent reductions took place, stood at about $300 billion annually. Additionally, the cost estimates, even at the low end, are based on worst-case scenarios. Actual costs may be less than expected.

Of course, the costs of greenhouse gas reduction must be balanced against the benefits. The most obvious is a slowing and perhaps a reduction of global warming. Businesses will also benefit in the long run from using machinery with greater energy efficiency, because reducing the use of fuel will help lower operating costs. To top it off, many of the greenhouse gases implicated in global warming are also responsible for other environmental problems. Reductions in emissions could help abate acid rain and deadly ozone depletion and reduce the particulate pollution that claims about sixty thousand lives in the United States every year.

One of the biggest obstacles inhibiting attempts to reduce greenhouse gas emissions comes from the developing world. Nations such as China and India want to draw upon their coal reserves as a means for industrialization. In doing so, they believe they are following the path to development and wealth taken by Europe and North America in years past. They want a share of the prosperity industrialization can offer, and they do not believe they should be hampered in doing so by environmental concerns that did not hinder the development of the older industrial nations. But this approach overlooks two important factors. First, in past decades the environmental degradation caused by the use of fossil fuels went unrecognized. The industrial nations acted out of ignorance. Does that mean nations of today should ignore our painfully acquired knowledge and recklessly adopt a hazardous course?

Second, India and China are populated by two billion people, more than lived in the entire world during early industrialization. Processes that worked a century ago are now hopelessly outmoded. To produce even one quarter of the developed world's standard of living would require the developing nations to vastly outstrip America and Europe in the use of coal, augmenting the amount of carbon dioxide reaching the atmosphere. This is a direct route to global ruin.

One way to avoid that problem would be for developed nations such as the United States and Japan to provide the funding and technology necessary for more efficient energy production. Such technology already exists. In the United States, for example, the production of electricity is 50 percent more efficient than it was in 1950. Exporting high-tech equipment to developing nations for energy production could also help to overcome their reluctance to cooperate in reducing carbon dioxide emissions.

To halt global warming, we need to cut carbon dioxide emissions by as much as 80 percent, methane emissions by up to 20 percent, and nitrous oxide emissions by as much as 85 percent by 2020; eliminate chlorofluorocarbons by 1995; and halt deforestation by 2000 and reforest an area roughly the size of California, Washington, and Oregon combined. Even if we accomplish these goals, mean global temperatures are likely to continue to rise two or three degrees by the middle of the next century before tapering off.

The time has come for decisive leadership committed to constructive change. We are in the eleventh hour, faced with the challenge not of stopping global warming and the damage it will bring—it is too late for that—but of trying to limit the warming and the damage. Presently the Clinton administration is attempting to initiate measures that will reduce carbon dioxide emissions to 1990 levels. However, congressional opposition to some of the stronger measures the administration sought during its first year has hobbled attempts at significant reductions. While it is impossible to predict the future of our nation's environmental policy, continued public response and outcry *will* increase the likelihood that beneficial changes will be implemented.

Chapter Nine

Population:
the Press of Humanity

Autumn came to Ireland moist and mild in 1845, perfect weather for the rapid growth and spread of *Phytophthora infestans*, the late potato blight. This fungus infects the leaves, stems, and roots of potatoes. In 1845 it was as yet unrecognized, and it would remain so for another fifty years, but its effects that year on the one crop upon which Ireland's laboring class depended were clear: The potato crop failed, as it did for the rest of the decade.

The result was a subsistence crisis. Ireland's population had exploded during the previous century and a half, from about 2 million people in 1700 to 8.2 million in 1846. Despite this rapid growth, everything seemed fine. After all, the Irish had this relatively new American miracle food, the potato, which had been a staple for about a century.

But any people dependent upon a single food source stand on the brink of destruction, as the Irish discovered. Between 1846 and 1851, deaths caused by the famine stood between 1 million and 1.5 million. John Mitchel, an Irish freedom fighter and journalist, described what he saw of that catastrophe during a trip across Ireland in the 1840s: ". . . sights that will never wholly leave the eyes that beheld them, cowering wretches almost naked in the savage weather, prowling in turnip fields, and endeavoring to grub up roots which had been left, but running to hide as the mailcoach rolled by: groups and families, sitting or wandering on the highroad, with failing steps, and dim, patient eyes, gazing hopelessly into infinite darkness and despair. . . . in front of the cottages, little children leaning against a fence when the sun shone out—for they could not stand—their limbs fleshless, their bodies half-naked, their faces bloated yet wrinkled, and of a pale greenish hue—children who would never, it was too plain, grow up to be men and women."

Although economists and historians can, and probably

Houses seemingly stacked atop one another are common sights in many Third World cities, especially along rivers. Overcrowding and inadequate or nonexistent sewage treatment fouls waters used for bathing, washing, and, sometimes, drinking. Floods can also devastate these makeshift developments, resulting in appalling casualties. (facing page)

will, debate endlessly over the causes and ramifications of the Irish potato famine, several things are clear: The population grew too rapidly; the staple food crop failed; at least one million people died of starvation, disease, and the rigors of emigration undertaken to escape the famine; the population dropped; and the famine resulted in a public-policy quagmire.

The Irish at least had an escape route. They could leave Ireland for more prosperous nations, such as the United States and Canada. Into the 1850s, as many as 250,000 people a year did exactly that. But today, as the world population grows, fewer and fewer places remain as sanctuaries for the poor and disenfranchised.

The United Nations, after a 1993 study of population trends, predicted that the world's population will stand at 11.5 billion by 2100. However, that presumes that population growth will decline in many nations as a result of family planning. If present rates of growth continue, the world population will reach 10 billion by 2030, 20 billion by 2070, and 40 billion by 2110. At these rates, what will happen to humanity if crop production begins to level off and decline as a result of global warming? What will the increased numbers eat? Where will they live?

Demographers—people who study population distribution—are already discovering patterns of emigration from areas of overpopulation and hunger to areas of wealth and potential, that is, from the developing world to the industrial nations. People around the globe already feel the strains of population movement.

The world's population is growing by 95 million yearly. By the end of the 1990s, more than half the world's developing nations may be unable to produce enough food to feed their citizens. Fuelwood, the primary source of domestic fuel in the developing world, will be unavailable to half the people who need it by the year 2000.

In attempting to understand the threats posed by overpopulation, environmentalists use predictions of population growth based on present trends. Because these predictions involve many variables, it is impossible to state with certainty exactly where human numbers will stand at the end of the next one hundred years. But uncertainty in numbers makes population growth no less serious; it is an issue humanity cannot afford to ignore.

Although these threats are discouraging, they are not foregone conclusions. They will become realities only if humankind fails to heed the warnings of overpopulation. Ideally, humanity will meet the challenge of population growth, and every prediction that follows will be proved wrong. That is the goal of the forecasting that comes from the environmental community: Environmentalists always hope that society will prove them wrong, initiating laws, regulations, and social behaviors that will reverse the conditions that lead to environmental degradation.

The human population is exploding after millions of years of relative stability. Our earliest human ancestors probably never numbered more than five million at any one time. Then, approximately ten thousand years ago, after the development of agriculture around the world, the population began to grow. Two thousand years ago, the number reached 300 million. By 1650, it stood at 500 million. Only 150 years after that, in 1800, the population reached its first billion, alarming Thomas Malthus, the British economist who predicted that humanity would soon overrun the globe and fall into famine. But until the past few years, our ability to produce crops continued to outpace our ability to reproduce. The Industrial Revolution and the technological miracles it yielded enhanced our ability to survive in greater and greater numbers.

Of course, the larger the population, the more rapidly it can grow. While it took millions of years for humanity to number one billion, we reached the second billion in less than 150 years, just before 1950. That number has already more than doubled. World population presently stands at 5.7 billion and is growing at almost one billion people per decade. Most of the growth occurs in Africa, Asia, and Latin America, areas often too poor to provide basic services for such masses of people.

Human overpopulation creates problems at every level of society, posing a threat to humanity, to life as we know it, and to the potential for a better life. Each additional person adds an increment to the demand on the environment. Each person's demand is multiplied to varying degrees by the person's affluence and by the environmental impact of technologies involved in production and consumption. The high population densities of large cities overwhelm water supplies, sanitation services, and waste-disposal systems. The rapid pace of population growth leaves little time to promote environmental safeguards or to introduce new technologies. Solving environmental problems becomes more difficult and more expensive when populations grow quickly. The steadily increasing burden of growing populations can eventually overload natural systems, such as rivers, lakes, and coasts already beleaguered with pollution, causing their collapse.

In 1985, only eleven cities in the entire world numbered more than ten million people. By 2000, an estimated two dozen cities will reach that level of population. Urban growth threatens the developing world by jeopardizing the croplands that developing nations need to feed swelling populations. As cities grow they convert agricultural lands and wildlands to industrial and residential use; take up increasing amounts of water and energy; and concentrate air and water pollution in small areas, creating toxic hot spots and overwhelming natural restorative processes, such as the filtering ability of wetlands. Since the 1960s, Egypt has lost 10 percent of its prime farmland to cities. The United States loses two million acres of farmland to urban sprawl each year. According to *The State of the World 1987*, between 1980 and 2000 urban expansion in the developing world will overrun more than nine million hectares. (A hectare, pronounced "heck-tar," is a standard unit of land measurement equal to about 2.47 acres.)

Rapid urban growth brings with it not only economic and social problems, but also a variety of health hazards. Crowded conditions nurture the spread of diseases such as tuberculosis and viral infections. Increases in water pollution also raise the incidence of disease. Today drinking-water pollution is linked directly to the deaths of 10 million to 25 million people yearly. India loses 73 million workdays and about $1 billion annually because of water-related illness.

Polluted waters cross international boundaries. Tijuana, Mexico, on California's southern border, is home to one million people, twice the number its wastewater treatment plant can accommodate. On some days, 43 million gallons of raw sewage pour from the city into the Pacific Ocean, eventually reaching California's beaches. Illness as a result of beach pollution has frightened people away from towns such as Imperial Beach, California, where beach-business profits are down 50 percent. In 1998, Tijuana will open a new wastewater treatment plant, but by then the town's population will near two million, exceeding the new plant's capacity.

About 70 percent of urban dwellers breathe unhealthful air at some time. In Latin America, chronic respiratory illness affects about 2.3 million children, and polluted urban air affects some 100,000 elderly bronchitis sufferers. Lead—pumped into urban areas by the combustion of fossil fuels, particularly in motor vehicles—affects vast numbers of inner-city residents all over the world, including the United States, where inner-city children show elevated levels of the metal in their blood. In Mexico City, home to one of the world's worst cases of air pollution, at least 50 percent of newborns possess blood lead levels high enough to cause mental or physical impairment.

Population growth creates a heavy demand for energy, speeding the drain of energy resources. Even theoretically renewable resources such as fuelwood can be wiped out by overuse. Nonrenewable resources, such as fossil fuels, are certain to run out as populations grow. Commercial energy consumption rose 22 percent in developing nations from 1980 to 1985. Half the increase was needed just to maintain per capita energy consumption as the population grew by 11 percent. In 1989, the developing world was consuming three times the amount of commercial energy it had used twenty years before. By 2025, it is likely that energy consumption in developing nations will have to double to meet the energy demands of increasing numbers of people. The burgeoning use of fossil fuels will intensify air and water pollution as well as associated health hazards.

Providing fresh water for human needs becomes increasingly difficult as populations grow. Although only 1 percent of the planet's water can be tapped for human use, that seemingly minuscule amount could provide for 20 billion people—if it were evenly distributed around the globe. Of course, it is not. Most of Africa, Northern Asia, and Australia fall victim to periodic water shortages. Even the American Midwest, the nation's breadbasket, is a relatively arid part of North America. Crops rely on irrigation water drawn from huge natural underground reservoirs, but this water is being taken out far faster than rainfall and other natural sources can replenish it. As midwestern and western cities grow, they put increasing demands on this diminishing water supply, creating a potential source of political conflict as agricultural interests find they must share their water supply with growing urban centers. Water demand is increasing worldwide, too. By 2000, about half of all nations will have doubled their 1970 water consumption. By 2025, water supplies in some twenty-five developing nations are likely to be shared among so many people that only minimum per capita needs will be met.

About 80 percent of freshwater consumption goes to agriculture. This increases the importance of freshwater reserves because as populations grow, food production must keep pace with them. But even this is not happening. From 1979 to 1987, cereal production per person declined in fifty-one developing nations, including twenty-five African and seventeen Latin American nations. In Africa south of the Sahara, population growth already is outstripping agriculture's ability to increase crop production through technological improvements. Although food production doubled between 1950 and 1980, the population tripled. If human fertility in Africa does not slow by 2000, half of the forty-six African nations south of the Sahara, unable to grow or import enough food, will find it impossible to feed their people.

Burgeoning human populations force farmers—particularly subsistence farmers, who seek to produce food for themselves and their families—into marginal croplands, such as steep slopes, as prime farmland is rapidly consumed. In Java, this has led to erosion on half of all farmlands, a condition that is likely to grow worse if the nation's population continues to grow, as experts anticipate. Moreover, when forests are cleared for crops, fuelwood grows scarce and farmers turn to burning manure. This reduces the amount of manure avail-

Decades of overgrazing have taken their toll in this area around Arivaca Creek in southern Arizona. First to suffer from overpopulation are land and water, two critical resources necessary for survival. Around the world, we are losing both on a grand scale, and neither can be replaced or quickly repaired.

able for use as fertilizer and leads to declines in crop yields. Around the world, lack of manure for fertilizer results in an annual loss of about twenty million metric tons of grain.

Erosion and other forms of land degradation, including wind and water erosion, pollution, and nutrient exhaustion, have diminished the productivity of an estimated 1.2 billion hectares since 1945—more than 10 percent of the planet's vegetated land surface. During the same period, the world's population has doubled, increasing the demand for food and fuel. This increase itself causes further degradation of productive land, including overgrazing, deforestation, and pollution. Cultivation of steep land and overgrazing of pastures augment the erosion that sweeps away an estimated 1 billion tons of topsoil yearly.

While populations in the developing world are rapidly expanding, growth in the industrial world is slowing. Fertility in most of the developed nations, such as England, Canada, and the United States, has leveled off to an average of 2.1 offspring per woman; in other words, births are nearly at replacement level, in which only enough children are born to replace their parents. For the United States, this is an improvement on the average of 3.7 births per woman that prevailed in the mid-1950s.

Despite downturns in the birth rates, the populations of the developed nations will continue to grow for a few decades because a large segment of the present population is young and has not yet had children. Emigration from over-crowded developing nations will also bloat the developed world. The United States, for example, grows by three mil-lion people yearly. This may seem quite manageable. However, at the present time, although they make up less than 25 percent of the world's population, people in devel-oped nations use about 75 percent of all raw materials and energy, create 75 percent of the world's solid wastes, and pro-duce 55 percent of the atmospheric gases involved in global warming. During the 1980s, the U.S. population grew by about 22 million. The energy demands of those 22 million are equal to those of 55 million Japanese, or 150 million tropical South Americans, or 530 million West Africans, or 660 million Southern Asians. If this level of resource con-sumption does not change in the years ahead, the 150 mil-lion people moving to or born into the developed world dur-ing the next thirty years will be the environmental equiva-lent of 4.5 billion people living at the level of citizens of India.

About 95 percent of the world's population growth—some 87 million people yearly—occurs in the developing nations, where today's 4.2 billion people are expected to approach 8.2 billion by 2025. Experts predict that Latin America's popula-tion will double by the same date; Asia's will grow 60 per-cent, reaching 4.5 billion despite a rapidly falling birth rate; and those of the Near East and North Africa will more than double to 562 million, leaving sixteen of the region's nine-teen nations unable to feed their people. The U.N. Food and Agriculture Organization (FAO) estimates that by 2000, thirteen Latin American and Caribbean nations will be unable to produce enough food for their people using present agricultural techniques. This area is already plagued by such population-related problems as pollution: About 81 million Latin Americans live in cities in which air is polluted almost all the time.

As social and economic predicaments in the developing world grow increasingly desperate, governments may institute reform. As Patricia Waak states in *Population Policy: Social Realities, Prospects, and the Three Ecos*, a 1991 publication of the National Audubon Society's Population Program: "Almost all population policies are formulated when a government reaches the decision that rapid growth conflicts with its goals for social and economic development and that it will not be able to respond to the needs of its citizens without firm population reduction measures." This is reflected in the fact that the nations in the direst straits are also making the most progress in stabilizing population growth.

Population growth is not just a human issue. It also represents a danger to the natural world. The International Union for the Conservation of Nature and Natural Resources—World Conservation Union (IUCN) recently studied forty African and Asian nations and found that in the ten countries that have lost the greatest amount of natural habitat (an average of 85 percent), people were living in densities of 1,888 individuals per square kilometer. In the ten nations that have lost the least amount of natural habitat (still a sizable average loss of 41 percent) the human density on average was 294 people per square kilometer.

Of course, it does not take statistical analysis to show that more people means less natural habitat. We in the twentieth century have seen firsthand what happens when a human tidal wave sweeps across the Earth—since 1900 the world has lost an estimated 50 percent of its wetlands; some 21,800 species faced extinction in 1989, including one in every thirteen plant species and one in every ten mammal and bird species; and tropical rain forests are falling at the rate of about 42 million acres yearly.

Every year, an estimated 17 million hectares of tropical rain forest are cut down worldwide. Asia is lopping down more than 1 percent of its forest yearly. Growing populations demand that more forest land be converted into cropland, and, since tropical soils usually produce crops for only two or three years before running out of nutrients, new farms must constantly be cleared from the forest. Biologist Norman Myers, quoted in *The Nature of Growth*, a 1991 publication of the National Audubon Society's Population Program, esti-

Tourists strike out along a rain-forest trail on the Caribbean island of St. Lucia. Rain forests are vast biological "farms," teeming with life. But they are being destroyed at the rate of some forty-two million acres a year, mostly for cropland and pasture.

mates that three-fifths of tropical deforestation results directly from small-scale landless or near-landless cultivators clearing new land for subsistence. By the end of the decade,
Myers says, this clearing will account for 75 percent of tropical deforestation. Commercial logging and ranching, which
Myers says presently account for 21 percent and 12 percent
of tropical deforestation respectively, will continue to diminish the world's forests. Presently, the world's protected areas
cover about 6.5 million square kilometers. If human population reaches the U.N. estimate of 11.5 billion in 2100, the
increase will require development of nearly half of the
presently protected lands.

In addition to demand for cropland, demand for fuelwood
is rising with population. As much as two-thirds of the
world's human population depends upon wood for heat and
cooking. Ninety percent of all African households use wood
for cooking. As wood around cities in developing nations is
cut, people must travel farther to find fuel. A 1985 study
revealed that between 1975 and 1982, urbanization contributed to the loss of 15 to 65 percent of the closed-canopy
forests lying within seventy miles of India's nine largest
cities. One reason for forest attrition was cutting for fuelwood.

Some Third World cities are surrounded by rings of deforestation that extend for several miles. In the Sahel—the
central part of Africa lying just below the Sahara—the
remaining trees can provide fuel sustainably for about 21
million people, but the region is already home to about 40
million. Fuelwood consumption there is estimated to exceed
tree growth by 30 percent. In India, consumption exceeded
growth by 70 percent in the early 1980s. In Ethiopia, consumption stands at 150 percent of growth.

An estimated 80 percent of the deforestation occurring in
developing nations is caused by population growth. At the
current rate of deforestation, by 2010 tropical forests will survive in only four of the seventy-six nations that today possess them. Deforestation is not limited to the tropics, however. Economic enticement is driving vast logging projects
wherever forests grow. Canada and Russia, holders of the
largest remaining expanses of forest in the Northern

Hemisphere, including the tallest trees on Earth, are in the process of liquidating their forests. Alberta, Canada, has sold virtually all its trees to loggers. British Columbia, with little or no input from the public, has sold vast stretches of ancient forest to Miller-Bloedal, a timber company in which the province owns stock. Canada will likely log most of its billion acres of forest within the next few decades.

Among natural environments, even the ocean does not escape unscathed. Coastal pollution will intensify as population grows, because coasts are the focus of human development. Presently, 60 to 70 percent of the world's population— as many as 3.8 billion people—live within seventy miles of an ocean coast. Thirty of the world's forty largest cities lie on or near a coast.

As people concentrate along ocean shores, so does their pollution. Pollution and development threaten to destroy coastal waters used as nurseries by 90 percent of the world's fish catch. Already many fish species are declining from the onslaught of pollution, development, and overfishing that results from increased demand for seafood. The hope of past decades that the oceans would feed the world has collapsed as fish populations have shown themselves more vulnerable to overfishing than scientists as recently as the 1950s guessed.

As human populations continue to expand around the globe, the need for food, water, and energy will surge, and humanity will claim an increasingly large portion of the Earth's plant and animal production. Presently, humans each year use about 40 percent of the planet's plant growth, including agricultural crops and such natural resources as trees and wild fruits and nuts. If the population doubles in the next century, will the Earth withstand human appropriation of some 80 percent of all plant production? The impact on forests and grasslands and the effect on the cleanliness of air and water will be staggering. Human use of fossil fuels will increase the amount of pollutants pumped into the air by hundreds of thousands, if not millions, of tons. These pollutants are the same ones that many scientists believe produce global warming, acid rain, and ozone depletion.

While the Earth will survive this destruction and pollution, many wildlife species—millions, in all likelihood—will not. And how these changes will affect humanity is nearly impossible to predict. As all creatures do, we rely on the planet's remaining stable so that we can continue to live as we do. Change the Earth too much—its array of species, air, water, and plant life—and it may turn into a place that will no longer sustain our present way of life.

We have nearly reached the limit of food production using current technology. In the future, unless we find means for increasing crop production, we will have to find ways to conserve crops.

The Earth has enough fresh water for an estimated 20 billion people, but this water is not evenly distributed. To provide water for that many people, nations rich in water would have to share it with more arid countries. This would mean finding ways to transport water, which could prove a logistical nightmare.

As for greenhouse gases, a by-product of our energy use, no one knows how much carbon dioxide, the most common greenhouse gas, can go into the atmosphere before climates go awry. To avoid finding out by firsthand experience, the Intergovernment Panel on Climate Change, an international agency that monitors factors involved in global warming, concluded that the world needs to reduce carbon dioxide emissions by 60 percent, which means a sizable cut in the use of fossil fuels and fuelwood. Presently, the average yearly per capita production of carbon dioxide worldwide stands at 3.9 tons per person. To cut emissions by 60 percent would mean reducing that per capita level to 2.3 tons yearly. But if population grows to the 8 billion expected by 2025, each person will be limited to about 1.6 tons yearly. This will require extensive changes in energy use, technology, and lifestyle.

Combining these factors with potential population growth and other data has led to four widely varying estimates of the Earth's carrying capacity for humans (the variations reflect differences in data used): (1) less than 2 billion, if everyone adopts the living standards of the developed world; (2) less than 5.5 billion, suggesting that the Earth already stands at the edge of its carrying capacity, as shown by extensive ecological damage across the globe; (3) about 8 billion, provided that everyone adopts an adequate but not luxurious living standard; and (4) unlimited, because technology and market forces will protect against from disaster.

The last concept is sometimes called cornucopian, after the horn of plenty. It has little grounding in reality, but those who think of human populations as markets for goods and sources of profit seem to like it. This idea is closely allied to another view—that the problem is not really one of overpopulation, but of patterns of consumption. If people adopted different habits of consumption, this perspective says, the world could support more people. If we were wiser with our resources—for example, if we saved grain by eating it ourselves instead of feeding it to cattle, which require many pounds of grain to produce one pound of beef—we could feed many more people even if agricultural production remained at today's levels. However, as Clark LeBlanc points out in *The Nature of Growth*, a 1991 publication of the National Audubon Society's Population Program, ". . . irrespective of potentialities, overpopulation is 'defined by the animals that occupy the turf, behaving as they naturally behave, not by a hypothetical group that *might* be substituted for them.'" In other words, we have to look at the way people really act—the way they actually eat and breed and consume—to make intelligent estimates of the globe's carrying capacity for humans.

As the estimates indicate, no one really knows the Earth's carrying capacity. But perhaps more immediately important are the limitations of the countries that contain the planet's population. We see those limitations in the poverty and violence of our crowded inner cities, in the refugees who come to U.S. shores from Haiti, China, and Latin America, in the living skeletons that, seen on our TV screens, drag across the barren wastes of Ethiopia. Clearly, we will make large parts of the Earth unbearably miserable for humankind long before we exceed the planet's carrying capacity.

The key to stemming the surge in population and much future human suffering can be defined in two words— reduced fertility. Reducing fertility, that is, reducing the number of offspring couples produce, may not be as difficult as it sounds. The Population Information Program at Johns

Hopkins University suggests that fertility can be cut by making family planning available to all who want it; by encouraging later marriage and childbearing (which can have benefits for women's health and education); by encouraging breast-feeding, which can lengthen the interval between pregnancies; and by improving the status of women, because in many societies it is women rather than men who show the greatest interest in reducing pregnancies. Of these approaches, family planning is the most efficient and offers the most promise for both reducing population growth and, ultimately, elevating the status of women.

Since 1970, family planning has played a major role in bringing population growth to replacement levels in such nations as Cuba, Singapore, Hong Kong, Taiwan, South Korea, and Cuba. Nations that have reached a three-children per family average include Argentina, Chile, Colombia, North Korea, Panama, Sri Lanka, Thailand, China, and Jamaica. About 50 percent of families in developing nations were using family planning in 1990. If all unwanted births in developing nations were prevented, world population in 2100 might stop at 9.1 billion.

If no changes occur in the present rate of population growth and resource consumption, we can anticipate that by 2000 most tropical rain forests will be severely damaged or destroyed, thousands of species will disappear, 25 percent of the world's fresh water will be polluted, more than half of all developing nations will be unable to feed their people without expensive food imports, and the world's population will stand at 6 billion. In the thirty-five years that follow, under the same conditions, world population could close in on 10 billion, and twenty-five developing nations, including all of North Africa and all of the Near East except Turkey, would lack sufficient drinking water.

Within the United States, the will to solve the problem seems to be growing. The Clinton administration has reversed Reagan and Bush policies that cut funding for United Nations programs designed to help reduce world population growth. This stimulant to family planning offers promise for fertility reduction and may prove crucial to a better world in the future.

Chapter Ten

VISION FOR THE FUTURE

At the heart of environmental activism lies the conviction that we can change the course of public policy—that we can stop the destruction of ecosystems and stem the growth of population—by working together, transforming our concern about the environment into personal action.

You can become an environmental activist by bringing your concerns into the public arena and attempting to shape local, state, national, and even international policies. Major environmental decisions in the United States are made in state legislatures, state and federal agencies, and Congress. You can influence these decisions by supporting environmental and conservation organizations and by contacting politicians, government agencies, and the news media.

Contacting Politicians

Elected officials offer you, as a voter, an opportunity to help mold political action, including voting on important environmental bills. When environmental matters are being considered in your state legislature or in Congress, contact your representatives and let them know how you want them to vote. Although hard core opponents of your viewpoint are unlikely to be swayed, an undecided official can be moved by an outpouring of opinion from constituents. You can phone your state and congressional delegations and offer your opinion, but the best approach is to write a short letter outlining your concerns.

The Agencies

The U.S. Fish and Wildlife Service, Environmental Protection Agency, U.S. Forest Service, and other federal agencies with important environmental roles exert great influence on federal environmental policy. (The same can be said of state agencies, such as departments of natural resources; the methods outlined here for contacting federal

A volunteer sorts and ties up stacks of newspapers at a recycling drop-off in the nation's capital. Just the Sunday New York Times requires 8,000 pounds of paper, or about 75,000 trees. If Americans could recycle all of our newspapers, about 12 million tons a day, we could save millions of trees.
(facing page)

agencies work at the state level, too.) You can directly influence the policies set by these bureaucrats by offering your
viewpoint at public agency hearings, held to collect public
opinion before policies are initiated or new actions are
taken. You do not have to attend a hearing to express your
opinion—a letter to the agency will work as well.

To find out when a public hearing will be held, you can
call the appropriate federal agency. But a more convenient
means for learning about public hearings is the *Federal
Register*, which the federal government publishes Monday
through Friday and which is available in most major public
libraries. The *Federal Register* announces every agency's proposed, interim, and final regulations. It also lists executive
actions, which come from the White House. Most regulations cannot legally take effect until they are published in
the *Federal Register*, which is the official vehicle for telling
the public what the government plans to do, or wants to do.
The *Federal Register* provides an address to which you can
send your comments and tells you where and when the federal agencies will hold public hearings.

The *Federal Register* is particularly useful in April and
October, when it includes a unified agenda that outlines the
long-term plans of all the federal agencies, including the
schedule for upcoming issues. This will give you some idea
which future issues of the *Federal Register* will be particularly
important to you.

Conservation groups also publish newsletters that tell you
when agencies are soliciting comments on policy issues and
regulations. Local newspapers are good sources of this information as well.

The Media
As anyone who has been involved in an attempt to create
social or political change knows, the time comes when you
need to take your message to the public. Whether your message concerns a national or a local issue, you have several
venues from which to choose:

Letters to the editor: This is the easiest approach to a
newspaper, since papers usually have a letters column, and
you can simply write a letter and drop it in the mail.

Newspaper editorials: These generally appear on the same page as the letters to the editor or on the opposite page. If you think you have a topic that would make an interesting editorial, call the editor of your newspaper; if the editor seems sympathetic, suggest that he or she write an editorial on it. Offer to supply information. The alternative is to ask whether you may write an editorial yourself. This works best if you are a recognized expert on your subject.

Newspaper stories: If you are working with an issue or with events that seem genuinely newsworthy, call your local paper and ask to speak with a reporter. Try to find a reporter with a history of reporting on the issue with which you are dealing. Give your story to this reporter and offer to provide other sources of information, including the names of other people with whom you are working.

Radio: This is an excellent medium for getting your message across, particularly if you can get air time on a regular talk show. Unlike television, radio can offer you a lot of time to express your views. Call-in programs allow a thorough airing of opinion. As with newspapers, you need to call your local station and see whether a reporter or program host is interested in working with you. You can also propose simple items that can be carried on the radio news. Or you can offer to send in a taped public service announcement, which may be little more than a short message telling listeners about an important upcoming meeting or urging them to express their opinions at a public hearing.

Television: It is much more difficult to get access to TV than to newspapers or radio because TV journalists have far less on-air time available. However, if you are engaged in an activity or event that may provide interesting scenes, call a local TV station and ask to speak to someone at the assignment desk. You can also try speaking directly to a TV reporter. Offer your story. Be sure to do this far enough in advance of the event to allow the reporter the time needed to schedule camera crews and interviews.

Magazines: It is very difficult to place a feature story in a national magazine. However, there are many publications devoted to a wide range of environmental topics. Write to the magazines published by environmental groups, or to independent environmental publications such as the regional *High Country News*. This is an ideal way to reach people who are receptive to your message and concerns. You should not send a complete article. Instead, write a one- or two-page query letter that outlines your story and describes your credentials as a writer and send it to an editor on the magazine staff. If interested, the editor will contact you.

If you are not interested in political activism, you can still help by bringing environmental concerns into your daily life. All environmental problems result from our actions—some from our political actions and some from our individual actions. While we can try to influence politicians, we have more direct control over ourselves. Simple activities such as recycling, properly disposing hazardous wastes, and conserving energy and water can all help reduce the impact we as individuals have upon the environment. Individual actions are additive, and since so many of us crowd the planet, they can combine to achieve significant results.

Many conservation groups, including the National Audubon Society, publish how-to booklets describing daily measures that can help create a better environment. Some of these measures, such as ways to cut energy costs for home heating and cooling, will save you money. Most of these publications are free. Contact Audubon or any of the other large groups and find out which publications may be useful to you.

Finally, do not let the task wear you down. Very often environmental activism can be tough and depressing. Indeed, an entire field of psychology, called ecopsychology, is growing up around the problem of environmental discouragement. But we are not helpless, and we can effect social change. However, we do need unshakable resolve, because we are engaged in an endless endeavor. We are not race horses, striving toward a finish line. We are watchdogs, ever on guard.

California Condor, 1986
Narrated by Robert Redford

The story: When this program was broadcast in 1985, the federal government was preparing to capture the last of the wild condors, which numbered fewer than twenty, and place them in a captive-breeding program.

Update: The condors have done well in captivity. The population now stands at about sixty birds; since 1991, ten condors have been released into their former habitat in California, and the U.S. Fish and Wildlife Service is preparing to release condors on the north side of the Grand Canyon, offering the possibility of creating a second wild population.

The Mysterious Black-footed Ferret, 1986
Narrated by Loretta Swit

The story: The only known population of the black-footed ferret, a relative of the weasel that lives in prairie dog towns, was on the verge of extinction from distemper when this program was produced in 1985. The U.S. Fish and Wildlife Service captured all known surviving black-footed ferrets for a captive-breeding program.

Update: Like the California condors, the ferrets have done well in captivity, where they number more than three hundred. Since 1990, FWS has released more than two hundred into the wild, where the animals have begun breeding.

Galápagos: My Fragile World, 1986
Narrated by Cliff Robertson

The story: This program examines threats posed to the Galápagos Islands off Ecuador, which are among the last of the world's nearly pristine natural wonders. Here sea lions and native birds do not fear people and allow close contact by human visitors.

Update: Ecuador, which owns the islands, uses strict controls on tourists and their activities to ensure that the islands remain undamaged.

On the Edge of Extinction: Panthers and Cheetahs, 1986
Narrated by Loretta Swit

The story: Cheetahs and Florida panthers are both on the verge of extinction; their wild populations are very low and are jeopardized by inbreeding. The chief cause of mortality among Florida panthers, which number fewer than fifty animals, is collision with motor vehicles.

Update: Florida has built openings under the state highways upon which panther kills have been particularly common. The openings allow the cats to move about safely. The state is also developing a program for revitalizing the Everglades, the panther's habitat.

Common Ground: Farming and Wildlife, 1987
Narrated by Dennis Weaver

The story: This program looks at the ways agricultural use of pesticides and land affects wildlife.

Update: The Clinton administration is creating new regulations that will more carefully guide the use of agricultural pesticides.

Ducks Under Siege, 1987
Narrated by John Heard

The story: This program examines how the use of wetlands across the nation is affecting waterfowl populations, which have been declining for the past decade despite a massive and well-established waterfowl management program.

Update: No good news. In 1993, duck populations were setting new lows.

Wood Stork, Barometer of the Everglades, 1987
Narrated by Richard Crenna

The story: Because of its unique feeding methods, the wood stork provides a good measure of the health of the Everglades. A declining stork population is a clear sign that the Everglades ecosystem is in trouble.

Update: The wood stork population remains low throughout the Everglades, but Florida's plans to improve water flow to the Everglades offer hope for the bird and its habitat.

Whales!, 1987
Narrated by Johnny Carson

The story: "Whales!" provides an overview of the lives of some of the world's largest species, including the humpback whale. When the program aired, the International Whaling Commission, which monitors whaling activities, had initiated a worldwide ban on whaling.

Update: Japan, Iceland, and Norway are threatening to resume whaling of some species, such as the minke whale, despite the continued ban.

Messages from the Birds, 1988
Narrated by Martin Sheen

The story: By examining the link between migratory birds and various wetlands, this program shows how wetlands destruction in the United States could harm bird populations throughout the Western Hemisphere.

Update: The Clinton administration has issued new wetlands regulations, promising no net loss of wetlands, but whether or not the program will work remains to be seen.

Sea Turtles: Ancient Nomads, 1988
Narrated by Jane Alexander

The story: Sea turtles wander throughout the world's oceans, yet their life histories are only poorly known; the reptiles are threatened by development of the beaches on which they nest and by those who collect their eggs.

Update: In the late 1980s the National Marine Fisheries Service began requiring commercial fishing vessels in the Southeast to use special devices that free sea turtles trapped in nets, a measure that should save the lives of thousands of sea turtles yearly in the Gulf of Mexico and off Florida's Atlantic coast.

Sharks, 1988
Narrated by Peter Benchley

The story: Though the shark is feared as a dangerous predator, only about one hundred incidents of sharks attacking humans actually occur yearly, and only about one-third of these are fatal. In contrast, fishermen kill about 100 million sharks every year, putting some shark populations in jeopardy.

Update: In 1993 the National Marine Fisheries Service initiated new regulations offering protection to Atlantic coastal shark populations, which have become vulnerable to overfishing.

Greed and Wildlife: Poaching in America, 1989
Narrated by Richard Chamberlain

The story: This program focuses particularly on the serious threat poachers have posed to U.S. black bear populations, which the poachers have killed off to supply bear parts to Korea and other Asian nations that use them in traditional medicine. The program also demonstrates that illegal commercial hunting of wildlife has been widespread and is dangerous for many species, including grizzlies and other trophy animals.

Update: The federal government is continuing its undercover operations against poachers; on the international scene, the United States in 1993 threatened to bring trade sanctions against China and Taiwan because of their illegal trade in tiger and rhinoceros parts.

Crane River, 1989
Narrated by Leonard Nimoy

The story: This program investigates dam projects on the Platte River in Colorado, Wyoming, and Nebraska and the threat the projects have posed to sandhill cranes and a variety of endangered and threatened species that use the river.

Update: The Environmental Protection Agency killed the Two Forks Dam project, which posed the greatest threat, while the program was in production; since then, Nebraska has proposed another dam project that creates a similar threat to the integrity of the Platte.

Ancient Forests: Rage Over Trees, 1989
Guest Hosted by Paul Newman

The story: This program provides a look at the people and personalities involved in the logging of the Pacific Northwest's ancient forests.

Update: The Clinton administration has formulated new regulations to limit, but not stop, logging in the Pacific Northwest.

Wolves, 1989
Narrated by Robert Redford

The story: "Wolves" examines how the gray wolf was pushed to the edge of extinction in the United States and what is being done to help it recover.

Update: In the late 1980s, red wolves, extinct in the wild, were released by the U.S. Fish and Wildlife Service into national wildlife refuges, where they have been breeding successfully. The federal government is exploring plans to reintroduce wolves to Yellowstone National Park and parts of Arizona and New Mexico.

If Dolphins Could Talk, 1990
Guest Hosted by Michael Douglas

The story: This program illustrates the threats dolphins face from coastal pollution and from the use of purse-seine nets in the southern Pacific's tuna fishing industry.

Update: U.S. tuna canning companies have promised to sell only tuna caught without jeopardizing dolphins; however, purse-seine fishermen, who sell their tuna to other nations as well, continue to kill thousands of dolphins in their nets.

Arctic Refuge: A Vanishing Wilderness, 1990
Narrated by Meryl Streep

The story: This program examines the Arctic National Wildlife Refuge, which lies on the last stretch of undeveloped coast in northern Alaska. The Bush administration was pushing hard to open the area to oil and gas development, although prospects for an oil find were marginal and expected supplies would meet U.S. oil demands for only seven months at best.

Update: Congress has so far offered steadfast resistance to opening the refuge to drilling, but has not given the refuge status as a wilderness area, which would better protect it from unnecessary development.

Danger at the Beach, 1990
Guest Hosted by Ted Danson

The story: This program gives an overview of U.S. coastal pollution problems, spanning the nation from Boston Harbor to Puget Sound.

Update: Coastal pollution continues to be a major problem, but public interest is increasing, offering hope for a national cleanup effort.

Wildfire, 1990
Guest Hosted by James Woods

The story: "Wildfire" looks at the role of fire in forests and grasslands and examines the 1988 Yellowstone National Park fire, which some politicians called a disaster but many scientists viewed as part of a natural cycle.

Update: The Yellowstone fire seems to have had little effect on wildlife, and vegetation shows signs of early recovery.

Hope for the Tropics, 1991
Guest Hosted by Lauren Bacall

The story: This program reports on Costa Rica's plans for protecting its rain forests while also using them for economic development, including selective logging and iguana ranching.

Update: Costa Rica remains a conservation leader in Central America, but tropical rain forests continue to decline worldwide.

The New Range Wars, 1991
Guest Hosted by Peter Coyote

The story: Public grasslands, administered largely by the Bureau of Land Management and the U.S. Forest Service, have been leased to private ranchers since the 1930s, but show little sign of recovering from serious overgrazing that began late in the nineteenth century; this program investigates the federal grazing program and how it affects public grasslands.

Update: The Clinton administration is attempting to raise grazing fees, which have been kept at bargain-basement levels for decades, and require better management of federal grasslands. Unfortunately, the livestock industry's minions in Congress have been trying to block the new initiatives.

Great Lakes, Bitter Legacy, 1991
Guest Hosted by James Earl Jones

The story: Industrial and agricultural developments have abused the Great Lakes for nearly 150 years, leading to widespread pollution of the lakes, declines in commercial fish species, and threats against human health from toxins.

Update: The federal government is initiating new programs to stem pollution of the Great Lakes.

Mysterious Elephants of the Congo, 1991
Guest Hosted by Jane Fonda

The story: This program represents the first televised report on the elephants of the African rain forest, which are smaller than the better-known savannah elephants but just as vulnerable to poaching for ivory.

Update: Poaching of elephants for ivory continues on a small scale, but thanks to an international ban on the sale of ivory, no longer poses a threat to elephant survival.

Battle for the Great Plains, 1992
Guest Hosted by Jane Fonda

The story: The grasslands of the Great Plains, once the home of immense herds of hoofed animals such as bison, are now a rangeland for cattle and other livestock.

Update: Efforts to protect native prairie are gaining popular support; after years of struggle, conservationists are close to reaching an agreement with ranchers and Native Americans on the protection of the Osage Hills northeast of Tulsa, Oklahoma.

The Environmental Tourist, 1992
Guest Hosted by Sam Waterston

The story: Ecotourism—whose primary goal is to see wildlife and wildlands firsthand—is the fastest-growing segment of the tourism industry. It offers both promise for wildlife protection, because it gives economic value to wildlife, and danger, because large influxes of tourists can damage habitats and disrupt wildlife behavior.

Update: The developing world is showing a growing interest in protecting wildlife and wild places that offer sources of revenue. The problem is that ecotourists are fickle, and when they lose interest in a place the impetus for saving it may be lost.

Greenhouse Gamble, 1992
Guest Hosted by Leonard Nimoy

The story: "Greenhouse Gamble" looks at research pro-

jects designed to reveal how global warming may affect wildlife.

Update: Although global warming continues to be a controversial issue in both the scientific and the political arena, most scientists agree that global warming is an impending problem.

Sex, Lives, and Holes in the Skies, 1992
Guest Hosted by Andie MacDowell

The story: Two profiles, one of a family in Madagascar and the other of a family in New York City, show how the problem of overpopulation is addressed in different parts of the world.

Update: The Clinton administration is likely to restore funding for international family-planning programs, one of the best means for reducing population growth in the developing world, where growth is fastest.

Caribbean Cool, 1993
Guest Hosted by Lou Gossett, Jr.

The story: "Caribbean Cool" presents an often humorous account of conservationist Paul Butler's imaginative efforts to save rare birds in the Caribbean islands.

Update: Butler's programs are growing throughout the Caribbean.

Hawaii: Paradise in Peril, 1993
Guest Hosted by Richard Chamberlain

The story: This program looks at the threats agriculture and unbridled tourism pose to Hawaii's natural resources.

Update: Threats continue as resort development overtakes natural habitats and coastlines.

Backlash in the Wild, 1993
Guest Hosted by Arthur Kent

The story: This program examines the wise-use movement, an effort heavily bankrolled by big development interests, such as the logging industry, to undermine U.S. environmental protection laws.

Update: Polls show that the wise-use movement is gathering support.

APPENDIX B:
ADDRESSES FOR ENVIRONMENTAL ACTIVISTS

Congress

Contact your senator by writing:

The Honorable _____

U.S. Senate

Washington, DC 20510

Contact your representative by writing:

The Honorable _____

U.S. House of Representatives

Washington, DC 20515

Telephone your senators and representatives at 1-202-224-3121. You can also reach members of your congressional delegation at their home offices. Check local listings for these addresses and phone numbers.

Federal Agencies

Bureau of Land Management

U.S. Department of the Interior

18th and C Streets NW

Rm. 5600

Washington, DC 20240

Oversees more public land than any other agency, some 300 million acres, mostly in the West and Alaska; the lands are used for everything from grazing and mining to outdoor recreation.

Bureau of Reclamation

U.S. Department of the Interior

18th and C Streets NW

Washington, DC 20240

Manages Western dam projects for irrigation and drinking water, flood control, and electricity generation.

Department of Agriculture

14th Street and Independence Avenue SW

Washington, DC 20250

The parent agency of the U.S. Forest Service and Soil Conservation Service.

Department of the Interior

Interior Building

1849 C Street NW

Washington, DC 20240

The parent agency of the Bureau of Land Management, Fish and Wildlife Service, and National Park Service.

Environmental Protection Agency

401 M Street NW

Washington, DC 20460

Enforces many major environmental laws, including the Clean Water and Clean Air acts and various laws regulating the use of pesticides and other toxins. It shares with the U.S. Army Corps of Engineers the responsibility for protecting wetlands under the Clean Water Act.

Federal Energy Regulatory Commission

825 N. Capitol Street NE

Washington, DC 20426

Licenses the construction and operation of nonfederal dams and other hydroelectric projects.

National Marine Fisheries Service

Silver Spring Metro Center 1

1335 East-West Highway

Silver Spring, Maryland 20910

Responsible for the protection of marine resources, including whales, dolphins, sea turtles, various marine mammals such as seals and walruses, and commercial fish species; administers the Marine Mammal Protection Act, and for marine species, the Endangered Species Act.

National Oceanic and Atmospheric Administration

Silver Spring Metro Center 1

1335 East-West Highway

Silver Spring, Maryland 20910

Among various scientific activities, this agency monitors marine pollution and helps states protect their coasts.

National Park Service
Interior Building
P.O. Box 37127
Washington, DC 20013-7127
Administers the national parks and national monuments (including the White House) and coordinates the Wild and Scenic Rivers System and the National Trail System.

Office of Conservation and Renewable Energy
Department of Energy
Forrestal Building
1000 Independence Avenue SW
Washington, DC 20585
Administers the Department of Energy's energy conservation programs and conducts research on renewable energy sources.

Soil Conservation Service
P.O. Box 2890
Washington, DC 20013
Provides information to farmers and ranchers on pesticide and land use, including techniques for avoiding erosion.

U.S. Army Corps of Engineers
Office of the Chief of Engineers
Pulaski Building
200 Massachusetts Avenue NW
Washington, DC 20314
Plans and builds dams, locks, levees, and various harbor and canal projects, and shares with the Environmental Protection Agency the responsibility for protecting wetlands under the Clean Water Act.

U.S. Fish and Wildlife Service
Department of the Interior
18th and C Streets NW
Washington, DC 20240
The federal government's primary wildlife protection agency; administers the National Wildlife Refuge System; oversees implementation of the Endangered Species Act, guides other federal agencies in their responsibilities for listed species; implements the Migratory Bird Treaty Act, including the setting of waterfowl hunting seasons.

U.S. Forest Service
P.O. Box 96090
Washington, DC 20013-6090
Administers the nearly 200 million acres of national forests, including the sale of trees to logging companies; also administers the National Grasslands System.

BIBLIOGRAPHY

DiSilvestro, Roger. *The Endangered Kingdom: The Struggle to Save America's Wildlife*. New York: John Wiley & Sons, 1989.

———. *Audubon Perspectives: Fight for Survival*. New York: John Wiley & Sons, 1990.

———. *Audubon Perspectives: The Rebirth of Nature*. New York: John Wiley & Sons, 1992.

———. *Reclaiming the Last Wild Places: A New Agenda for Biodiversity*. New York: John Wiley & Sons, 1993.

Douglas, Marjory Stoneman. *The Everglades: River of Grass*. Atlanta: Mockingbird Books, 1947.

Douglis, Carole. "Images of Home." *Wilderness*, Fall (1993): 10–22.

Flavin, Christopher. "Slowing global warming." *State of the World*, 17-38. New York: Worldwatch Institute/Norton Press, 1990.

Foster, R. F. *Modern Ireland: 1600–1972*. London: Allen Lane, Penguin Press, 1988.

———. *The Oxford Illustrated History of Ireland*. Oxford: Oxford University Press, 1989.

Fox, Robert W., and Ira H. Mehlman, eds. *Crowding Out the Future: World Population Growth, U.S. Immigration, and Pressures on Natural Resources*. Washington, D.C.: Federation for American Immigration Reform, 1992.

Fox, Stephen. *The American Conservation Movement: John Muir and His Legacy*. Madison: University of Wisconsin Press, 1981.

Goldenberg, Jose. "How to stop global warming." *Technology Review*, November/December (1990): 25–31.

Graham, Frank Jr. *The Audubon Ark: A History of the National Audubon Society*. New York: Alfred A. Knopf, 1990.

Kunzig, Robert. "Earth on ice." *Discover*, April (1991): 55–61.

LeBlanc, Clark. *The Nature of Growth: An Audubon Population Program Survey of Human Population Growth and Biodiversity Resources*. Washington, D.C.: National Audubon Society, 1991.

Leffingwell, William Bruce, ed. *Shooting on Upland, Marsh, and Stream*. Chicago: Rand, McNally & Co., 1980.

Lillard, Richard G. *The Great Forest*. New York: Alfred A. Knopf, 1947.

Marshall, Alex. *State of World Population, 1992*. New York: United Nations Population Fund, 1992.

MacManus, Seamus. *The Story of the Irish Race*. Old Greenwich, Conn.: Devin-Adair Co., 1991.

Mitchell, John G. "A man called Bird." *Audubon*, March (1987): 81-104.

National Wildlife Federation. "Use the News to Protect Your Environment." Washington, D.C.: National Wildlife Federation, 1992.

———. "Watching the Watchdogs." Washington, D.C.: National Wildlife Federation, 1992.

———. "Your Choices Count." Washington, D.C.: National Wildlife Federation, 1992.

Ogden, John C. "The Wood Stork." In *The Audubon Wildlife Report 1985*, Roger DiSilvestro, ed., 458-470. New York, 1985.

Peters, Robert. "Effects of global warming on species and habitats: an overview." *Endangered Species Update*. May (1988): 1-8.

Sanders, Scott Russell, ed. *Audubon Reader: The Best Writings of John James Audubon*. Bloomington: Indiana University Press, 1986.

Schneider, Stephen. "Climate models." *Scientific American*, Vol. 256 (1987): 72-80.

————. "The greenhouse effect: science and policy." *Science*, (February 10, 1989): 771–79.

————. "The changing climate." *Scientific American*, (September 1989): 70–78.

Schroger, A. W. *The Passenger Pigeon: Its Natural History and Extinction*. Madison: The University of Wisconsin Press, 1955.

Trefil, James. "Modeling Earth's future climate requires both science and guesswork." *Smithsonian*, (December 1990): 28–39.

Waak, Patricia. *Population Policy: Social Realities, Prospects, and the Three Ecos*. Washington, D.C.: National Audubon Society, 1991.

————. *Choices, Responsibility, and Ethics in a Growing World of People*. Washington, D.C.: National Audubon Society, 1991.

Weatherford, Jack. *Native Roots: How the Indians Enriched America*. New York: Crown, 1991.

White, Robert M. "The great climate debate." *Scientific American*, (July 1990): 36–43.

Photo Credits

INDEX

Acknowledgments

Filmmaking involves extraordinary teamwork and collaboration. I often think of the friends and colleagues who have supported the Audubon Television Department's work during the past ten years. With regard to our flagship series, the *World of Audubon Specials* on TBS Superstation, I particularly want to thank:

• Ted Turner, whom I can never thank enough, because he has stood by Audubon Television programming through thick and thin, even when development interests have driven away advertisers.

• Russ Peterson, the former Audubon president who supported my early ideas for getting Audubon into television, despite the concern of those who feared that the Society's aggressive involvement in television would create much controversy.

• Peter Berle, Audubon's current president, who is both a terrific and supportive boss and a passionate environmentalist.

• My Audubon friends and colleagues, both on staff and on the board of directors, who generously give their time and expertise to our productions.

• My colleagues at Turner Broadcasting, led by Terry Segal, Pat Mitchell, and Thom Beers, without whom this series would not be possible.

• My donors for their inspiration, loyalty, and commitment.

• My colleagues at Audubon Productions, including Tom Belford, Caitlin Buchman, Claude Carmichael, Page Chichester (who took most of the photographs in this book), Dave Clark (who produced the two-hour special for which this book is a companion), Gray Coleman, Jonathan Diamond, Roger Di Silvestro (who wrote this book), Geoffrey Little, Frank Salerno, Delores Simmons, Dennis Sullivan, and Ruth Thomas. Our work in television with Turner Broadcasting would not be possible without these motivated, talented, and hardworking friends.

• Last, but not least, our producers, writers, editors, sound recordists, and cinematographers, without whose courage, creativity, dedication, and vision the Audubon TV Specials would not exist.

—Christopher N. Palmer